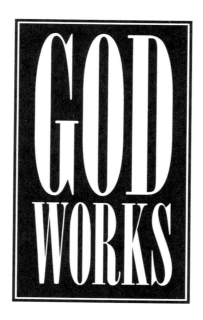

# YOUTH AND YOUNG ADULT MINISTRY MODELS...
# EVANGELISM AT WORK WITH YOUNG PEOPLE

Thomas K. Chu

Sheryl A. Kujawa

Anne Rowthorn

MOREHOUSE PUBLISHING

Morehouse Publishing
P.O. Box 1321
Harrisburg, PA 17105


All photographs are by Anne Rowthorn
Copy Editor, Lois Sibley
Art Editor, Linda daCosta Brooks

**A catalog record for this book is available from the Library of Congress.**

Printed in the United States of America

"God works in marvellous ways, countless wonders to perform."

—William Cowper (adapted)
The Hymnal 1982, #677

# Preface

The production of this book has been a truly collaborative effort. The indefatigable energy and perceptive skill of Dr. Anne Rowthorn who also did all the interviewing and the drafting gave this project much of its shape and creativity. Support for writing and production have been provided through the budget of the Ministries with Young People Cluster at the Episcopal Church Center with the assistance of the Standing Commission on Evangelism. Thanks should be extended to all the members of the commission for their support and encouragement during this process, and in particular to the Rev. Julia Easley for her counsel during the site selection process. I would also like to extend my sincere gratitude to all the people who made the visitations possible and who agreed to share their faith and ministry with us. It is our hope that *GodWorks* captures some of the commitment and the joy that was shared during the visitations. For these models to come together many young people and adults opened their hearts and minds to us and for their trust and support I am humbled. Consider this book as an offering that I hope will inspire and encourage your interest in ministry and evangelism with young people.

The Rev. Dr. Sheryl A. Kujawa
Episcopal Church Center
New York, New York
February 1997

# CONTENTS

# INTRODUCTION

U ntil now, no resource existed that shares models of evangelism that work with young people within the Episcopal Church. Though there was concern, those who wanted fresh ideas or wished to initiate new youth and young adult ministries could not get much help from us in terms of being handed one concise resource. With the publication of *GodWorks*, we trust that situation is changing.

The Episcopal Church Center staff members responsible for this project are the Rev. Dr. Sheryl A. Kujawa and Mr. Thomas K. Chu of the Ministries with Young People Cluster. The on-site interviewer and writer is Dr. Anne Rowthorn.

Through the presentation of eleven models of youth/young adult ministries already in operation, with pictures, formats, procedures, how-to ideas, tips for success, we now have some stories to share. No "pie in the sky" or book of "shoulds," this is intended to be a practical resource revolving around models of programs actually being carried out at various Episcopal churches, centers, universities and schools. These models include ministries with different approaches: peer evangelism/counseling, community models and congregational and diocesan models, models of residential campus ministries, and ministries to commuter students.

Each model is presented within its theological and cultural context. We have tried to be realistic, giving people credit for their gifts, and at the same time offering their stories as challenges to others. It was our intention to value each individual ministry for what it is and what is done, rather than suggesting that one approach will be helpful under all circumstances. We have attempted to present the difficulties of the ministries, and their limitations, as well as their strengths. Above all, we wanted the young people and their mentors at each location to speak for themselves and tell the stories of their lives and ministries in their own words. From the start we wanted to be clear that each of the models is evangelistic under a wide enough umbrella that would cover all. Thus our working definition of evangelism was as follows: *to evangelize means to help young people encounter the gospel, and recognize the presence of God in their personal and social histories.*

And who are the young adults we encountered in our travels? In a phrase, they are courageous people who touch the heart. They are Moselle Whitehead, a 21-year-old sophomore at the University of Buffalo, whose mother died when she was nine, and who remembers that she cried so hard, thinking, "I just want to go with her," but who learned "...when I got older I realized that life goes on and that I can be somebody." They are Louie Leung, a 20-year-old computer science major at Pace University, who came to New York City from Hong Kong five years ago, not speaking a word of English. "I didn't know anybody. I just sat in a corner. I couldn't say anything." They are people who are learning about the world beyond U.S. borders, like Ramsay Hoke, a 24-year-old graduate of the University of North Carolina, who spent a year in Costa Rica, "...a hard and lonely experience." He was robbed at gunpoint but nonetheless became convinced that "You can't gauge what's going on until you see the world in another context...it wakes you up." And we met people who are intent to change the world, like, Ericka Shells, a 17-year-old high school senior in Memphis. "The system is messed up and I want to change it. It's hard for people in the lower class to find a lawyer. I'm going to be a lawyer to help them." We met Eagle Scouts in Atlanta, who built playgrounds for young children in urban neighborhoods, like 17-year-olds Brian Yancy and Jeremy Stacy, peer counselors at Holy Innocents Episcopal School.

The young people who talked with us are idealistic and practical at the same time. They appreciate humor. They want a safe place, but not so protected that it shields them from asking the deep questions of life whose answers do not come easily. They want the community of the church or campus ministry, but they also want the freedom to throw it all out—all the values and beliefs passed to them by their families and significant elders. It is heady but hard. Young people are vulnerable. They appreciate adults who try to understand and do not judge them too harshly. What about sex, drug, and alcohol abuse? The Marshfield, Massachusetts young people illustrated that many of their peers are more concerned about their parents' abuse than their own. They are disturbed that adults in their world are not modeling responsible behavior.

Talking with the young people reminded us that a family's privileged, socio-economic status offers little protection against life's pressures; indeed that the pressure to succeed can be literally killing. Anorexia unchecked kills just as certainly as a bullet to the head in a drive-by shooting. Lack of economic and cultural resources are killers. They kill not only the body, but the spirit and a sense of wonder. At two public housing projects in Memphis, we got a taste of the world Jonathan Kozol's writes about in *Amazing Grace; The Lives of Children and the Conscience of a Nation*. Like Kozol, we were touched by the truly amazing grace of the children and their mentors. Grace and courage. To live in a world where there are few dependable maps to the future, under the shadow of a mushroom cloud with a volcano erupting underneath, takes courage, sheer courage. These young people have it. And along with it, the determination to make their lives make a difference.

Walter Bruggemann has said that one of the signs of new vision would be the emergence of new songs. Carefully, very quietly, incline your ear. Can you hear the music? The young people at St. Timothy's Church in Danville, California are making music, and their music, blended with the melodies of so many others, is echoing across the land. The sounds you pick up are notes of hope and expectation. May they touch your hearts and become your invitation to join the song.

# Five Boys and a Football

## URBAN COMMUNITY OUTREACH

No one at the Emmanuel Episcopal Center is "singin' the blues" even though Beale Street where W. C. Handy gave birth to the blues is just a few blocks away. Nor has the King been forgotten. The Lorraine Hotel where Martin Luther King, Jr. was assassinated April 14, 1968 is just a short distance in the other direction. It is both a reminder to Emmanuel Center's youth and young adults that theirs are not the only lives lived on the edge, and that the dream lives on.

The Emmanuel Center is located between two public housing projects, Cleaborn and Foote Homes in the south of Memphis, close to 'Ol Man Mississippi River. It is a graceland, an oasis, which, if it were not there, would give residents of the area a great deal to be blue about. "This is a drug-infested neighborhood," cites Ruthie Douglass, a mother of eight and grandmother of thirty-nine, who raised her children in the area. The strength of her assertion is questioned by the interviewer, so Mrs. Douglass states it more emphatically:

*Drug infested. Crack infested. The conditions are worse than they've ever been. It's all due to drugs. Everyone wants the quick dollar. People come into the community to sell drugs to elementary school kids....And the police know it's happening. They could stop it but they don't. Drugs are killing our kids.*

A shadow passes over her face. Her head drops; she pauses, then continues, slowly sharing the story of one of her sons:

*He's incarcerated now. It was drugs. You know, I had such strong hopes for him. He's very intelligent...but he got involved with the wrong crowd.*

The mother's anguish is felt around the small room. She continues,

*I write to him. I send him songs. He loves to hear songs and prayers. I send him all kinds of prayers.*

*We pray together on the phone. He's so special to me. He tells me...(pause)..."Momma, don't you worry."*

Ruthie's sister, Gladys, explains what drove her to move to a safer neighborhood:

*I had to keep the kids safe and it wasn't easy. I'd tell them to stay in the house or they'd get shot. I mean I had to keep them upstairs because I had drug people living next door to me. They were coming and going all night long. I'm not saying anyone would want to kill my kids, but with my next door neighbors in drugs I was afraid. No, terrified! I was terrified by the thought of drive-by shootings.*

Mack Gray, who admits to being "a retired gangster," picks up the conversation's thread:

*Do you understand that this is a totally drug-infested community? The kids carry pistols. You know how you used to carry notebooks to school? Now the kids carry guns. Why? Because they want everything and they want it now. $150 tennis shoes. Layaway? They never heard of layaway. They want it now and crack is how to get it.*

There are about 1,400 family units in the Cleaborn and Foote Homes. All residents receive some form of financial assistance from the government. The median education level is the ninth grade and most of the residents lack adequate education or marketable skills to be gainfully employed.

The amenities of the neighborhood include pathways connecting the buildings, grassy areas for children's games shaded by tall, leafy trees. On a good day one can see 15-year-old Rarecas Bonds demonstrating the flip. John Grisham, author of *The Firm*, was walking through one day looking for local kids for walk-on roles for the film version. He saw Rarecas and gave him a place on the silver screen. Rarecas and his friends spend their time playing touch football and basketball. They ride their bikes and hang around. Girls are less in evidence but when they pass through, they are noticed.

Other amenities include a store—Willie Moore's Grocery, in front of which drugs pass freely. There are also the two Vance Middle Schools—the old one, a red-brick 1930s issue, which is still standing with all its windows broken, and next to it the new school with very few windows. The new public library on the corner has even fewer. Vandalism control, the writer is told.

But people are not singing the blues, they are singing songs of hope and expectation, because of the Emmanuel Center and its total, comprehensive youth programs and community services. They are singing "Amazing Grace" because they see grace happening every day.

## The Emmanuel Episcopal Center

The Emmanuel Episcopal Center was established in September of 1989 as an outreach ministry of the Diocese of West Tennessee. The use of the building, an attractive brick colonial-style structure, has been redefined to keep pace with the changing constituency, places of residence of the church members, and the needs of the community. Originally, it was

PROCLAIMING JESUS CHRIST IN WORD AND DEED

EMMANUEL EPISCOPAL CENTER

EMMANUEL EPISCOPAL CENTER
604 St. Paul Avenue
Memphis, Tennessee 38126
901/523-2617

Grace Episcopal Church, established at the location in 1894. It was followed by Emmanuel Episcopal Church, which served the community for over forty years until most of its members had moved to other areas of the city and suburbs.

The center is well-equipped and includes the church, which also serves as a gym, and a large parish hall; meeting rooms; a kitchen; classrooms; a screen print shop; computer rooms; a lending library; and offices. Much of the equipment (computers, print shop machines, books, etc.) has been donated by the center's many friends, who also volunteer themselves and their skills.

The vision for the Emmanuel Center was that it would no longer be a church but a community center with a spiritual emphasis, and that a director and staff would be drawn together to create a strategy to empower individuals in ways that would raise them out of poverty and dependence into full participation in the mainstream of society. The Rev. Colenzo Hubbard, with a degree in social work, and eight and a half years experience in business management, was appointed the center's director with a mandate to create the program.

## Programs to Build Lives

The intention was that the Emmanuel Center would be a total community with programs and services for everyone of all ages and conditions of life running almost nonstop every day of the week. Programs are divided into four divisions: Youth-N-Action, Exodus, Overcomers, and Community Impact.

*Overcomers*, which serves mainly the homeless and unemployed, includes such services as alcohol and drug rehabilitation, emergency assistance, family sponsorship, job training and placement, legal assistance, and transitional housing.

*Community Impact* works with agencies, churches, and community organizations to sponsor community gatherings and emeregency assistance as well as holiday parties for the neighborhood. There are parent support teams, a Resident's Advisory Council, and rummage sales.

*Youth-N-Action* and *Exodus* between them cover everything touching on the lives of youth and young adults. Youth-N-Action and Exodus' programs run every day after school, some evenings, and vacations. Staffers, mostly from the immediate neighborhood, coordinate the divisions and, in the case of the youth/young adult programs, high school students serve on the staff as paid youth assistants.

*Youth-N-Action* targets children and youth between the ages of four and eighteen. It was the first cluster of programs established at the center. About 200 young people are actively involved in the following programs.

- **After School Activities.** All kinds of after school activities are offered, including: homework assistance, Bible study and chapel services, field trips, and recreation.

- **Cultural Enrichment.** Choir and art classes.

- **Job Placement.** Older youth are hired as group leaders providing supervision for younger participants, Most of them have grown up in the programs of the center. A training program in entrepreneurship provides young people with the experience of establishing and organizing small businesses. A screen print shop is located in the center, where youth are trained to design, print, and market T-shirts.

- **Organized Sports.** Year-round sports include basketball, baseball, football, softball, and Tee-ball. There are teams for youth of all ages.

- **Retreats.** Retreats are conducted for middle and high school youth throughout the year.

- **Spiritual Direction.** Bible studies are held twice weekly as well as chapel services on Friday afternoons.

- **Summer Camp.** The center sponsors an eight-week camp and overnight camps during the summer nights.

*Exodus* provides these programs in educational enrichment for people in pre-school to adult years:

- **Adult literacy.** Assistance in improving basic reading and writing skills, G.E.D. test preparation.

- **College Preparation.** Programs are offered to assist adults in earning associate degrees; also computer-assisted test preparation for high school students.

- **Computer Learning Center.** The center provides computer instruction on IBM and Macintosh computers and programs and computer-assisted instruction for all ages of pre-schoolers and youth.

- **Scholarship Tours.** Every year a scholarship tour is organized for high scholastic achievers. The tours have gone to Washington, Disney World and Cooperstown, New York. This year a trip to Colonial Williamsburg is planned. A minimum of a 3.0 grade point average is required for participation.

- **Emmanuel Scholars.** Academically talented students who would be helped by getting away are assisted in attaining scholarships to church schools and boarding schools. The staff also uses its influence to help students get accepted to Memphis's most academically rigorous high schools.

- **Homework Help.** After school, youth are assisted in completing their homework and taught constructive study habits.

- **Pre-School Activities.** The center's youngest children are taught socialization skills in preparation for entering elementary school.

- **Science Enrichment.** Science enrichment exposes youth to activities to enhance their interest in science. Activities include field trips, camps, and instruction by the staff of the local science museum.

- **Tutoring.** Tutoring is provided in math, reading, and science.

- **Vision Trips.** "Vision trips" are educational field trips designed to broaden the sights of youth and motivate them to want to excel in school.

Director Colenzo Hubbard, aware of the enormity of his task, realized that only a loving God could carry off the center's wide range of programs, turn around, and direct the lives of the people. "I was hired as the center's director, not a vicar or rector, but I couldn't hold myself back. I couldn't do it without God, without a worshiping community right at the heart of our work."

Thus, soon after coming to the Emmanuel Center, Father Hubbard initiated a new congregation. It was, in his words, "The only natural thing to do." It's name is St. Joseph's. Why? According to Colenzo, "St. Joseph wasn't Jesus' natural father. So many of the children here are fatherless. They are raised by others, by the Josephs who love them and care for them." He concludes, "Everything we do here honors God—whether we play basketball, or pool, whether we're painting T-shirts—sooner or later we talk about God."

## In the Beginning...

According to Roscoe McWilliams, an Emmanuel Center board member,

*This is a very dangerous area. Colenzo didn't have to come here. Unless you love kids you can't do this job. You can't do it for the money. Pay isn't a factor with Colenzo. He is unique. He could go anyplace in the USA and name his salary.*

Colenzo Hubbard became the Emmanuel Center's first executive director in 1989. He is a graduate of the University of Alabama with a degree in social work. At Alabama he was a football hero, playing on the Crimson Tide football team. He came to the priesthood after eight-and-a-half years as transportation manager for Ryder Truck Rental. Before coming to the Emmanuel Center, he directed evangelism and outreach ministries for an Episcopal church in Alabama.

He is blessed with a talented wife, Debra Hubbard, who has an M.A. degree in special education and has spent twelve years teaching in the Birmingham city schools. She is the director of the Exodus division. The Hubbards have two daughters, Charon, age 14 and Karin, age 11. The whole family works and volunteers at the Emmanuel Center.

An athletic star is particularly valued in an area where, if young men dream at all, it might be to make it in the sports world. Athletic expertise is just one of Colenzo Hubbard's qualifications, but it is an important one and served as a catalyst for the building of the community center.

Debra Hubbard explains that, "We began with a six-foot table and a phone. That's all. Then we bought a typewriter, which was promptly stolen." But the Hubbards are not the kind of people to be easily discouraged. They are also creative. After repeatedly painting over the graffiti that kept appearing on the center's doors, they decided that anyone who wanted to could place, not only a fingerprint, but whole handprints on the doors. Furthermore, the center would supply the paint. The graffiti stopped immediately.

"This is how we started the center," Father Hubbard explains: "I bought a football and went out to the same place every day after school and played with the kids. The first day five boys came and two of them are still involved. I did this for three weeks and then I asked the kids to a Bible club. My idea was to get to know the kids personally and through them their parents. I wanted to grow the ministry with them and stay with them through high school. I felt that if I had five to ten years of influence on their lives that they could make it.

"So we played ball and I followed the children home. I got to know their parents. You understand that most of them were completely unchurched, but they were willing to have Bible studies in their homes. At one point we had sixteen Bible study groups going.

"We had spaghetti suppers and invited the people—virtually no one had ever been in the building before—and I wanted them to feel comfortable about coming in.

"I'm not interested in just being the director of a community center. It's the spiritual dimension....*Any* effort to get people out of poverty has to have a spiritual commitment.

"I grew up in poverty but I never want to be so high that I'm not involved with people, I always want to be out there playing basketball with the kids.

"I think God has been preparing me all my life for this job. It fits. I've learned that if you have a willingness to serve, God will reward you with a fulfilling life.

"For me, my work is incomplete until I get the people into a worshiping community. God wanted us to create an environment where a person can sleep in an abandoned building on Saturday night and come to church on a Sunday morning."

Debra continues: "Everyone here has value. They just don't have some of the resources they need. Now they're behind. I want these kids to gain the skills they need to catapult them into the twenty-first century. I hope we can advocate for the things we know they'll need to compete—math, science, writing, and communication skills....They can attain it, if they can visualize it."

And finally, according to Hubbard, "I want this center to bring a message of hope to everyone in need. I want this center to be where adults can come, where kids can be kids, in a place filled with the sounds of learning."

## Dedrick Gray, One of the Five Boys With a Football

Dedrick Gray, age 15, is a ninth grader at Booker T. Washington High School. He is one of the five boys Colenzo Hubbard reached out to when he first came to the Emmanuel Center. They played football together after school and then Dedrick brought Colenzo home to meet his mother. She subsequently became a volunteer and then a staff member of the Emmanuel Center. According to Dedrick,

*I come to the center because they teach about God in a fun way. In the future I'd like to be a professional basketball player. If I don't make it I'll have computers to fall back on.*

## Portraits of Success

**Ms. Phyllis Daniels and her family**—Phyllis; Antonio, age 18, eleventh grade; Ericka, age 17, twelfth grade; and Mario, age 15, a middle school student. Phyllis was born in the neighborhood and has lived here all her life. Antonio was one of the five boys with whom Father Hubbard initially started playing football after school. Both he and Ericka are employed by the center as youth assistants. Ms. Daniels talks about why the center is important to her family:

> I'm blessed. My children are growing up doing the things they want to do. Because of the center, they're seeing things I've never seen. They're doing things I never did...Orlando, camping....They go to the movies.

> The Emmanuel Center keeps them out of trouble. They learn. They do their homework every day. They play basketball. If the center wasn't here they'd be in trouble. Here children have a place to go. There should be centers like this everywhere.

> When the center first opened, Father Hubbard invited the children and their parents to come over. He said, "Just come and enjoy yourself." He puts kids first. That's why the center's big now. He makes sure they have something to do every time they come to the center.

> When he started out, he came knocking on doors and the people opened up to him. He said prayers in people's houses. When I was sick he said a prayer. He had prayer meetings in the house.

> I'm proud of my children. Ericka's graduating this spring and whatever she decides to do, I'll be right behind her because she's my child...She's my daughter.

Ericka continues, "I'm going to college and I'm going to law school. I met a judge who said he'll help me. I'm not shy...never have been. The system is messed up and I want to change it. It's hard for people in the lower class to find a lawyer. I want to be a lawyer to help them."

**Mrs. Betty Isom,** director of Community Impact, mother of eight children, six of whom participate in Emmanuel Center programs, says:

> When I started eight years ago, I was a volunteer from the neighborhood. Duke (now age 12), started coming. He came and played with the kids every day after school. Then Father Hubbard had Bible study in my house every week. I invited other people in the unit. Eventually their kids started coming to the center too. Then Father Hubbard got me into literacy counseling. I had a tutor who helped me with speech and writing, twice a week for three years. They [Father Hubbard] realized my administrative abilities and offered me a job.

Betty organizes the Christmas adopt-a-Child program. She keeps a wish list and when children and adults want anything, "toys, clothing, color TVs, living room sets, boom boxes, bikes, teddy bears," she tries to get the article and make the wishes come true. Many of her own wishes have come true. She is doing well and so are her children.

**Ms. Glitters Fletcher and Alexander,** age 5, reports that:

> I used to be an addict...cocaine. I said to the Lord, "I can't do it any more. I've got to stop it." And God did stop it. He made me stop it. I stopped for my life and my soul. Now I'm living a new life and I don't do the things I did any more. I do baby-sitting in my house. They call me "Mother of the 'hood."

> I want my son to finish school, get a college education and make up his mind what he will do with his life.

Alexander adds, "I want to be a doctor because I want to help people get well."

**Leila Robinson and her parents.** Coach Carl Robinson teaches a range of sports at the Emmanuel Center, afternoons and weekends: Tee-ball, softball, baseball, football, basketball, and pool. Leila's mother, Vivian, is very concerned to help her children succeed. Leila is a high school freshman. She is an excellent student and plays basketball.

Leila introduces herself:

*Last year I made straight As in pre-algebra. This year I'm taking algebra along with my other subjects. School's pretty easy for me. I'm going to be a biologist because I like working with the many things that have to do with life. I'd also like to be a professional basketball player but maybe that's just a dream.*

*I come here every afternoon and most evenings...except when I'm playing basketball. Almost all my friends are here.*

Leila's mother, Vivian, believes that no child is too young to start coming to the center. She is pleased that her three-year old daughter, Carlnesha, is already involved: "Teen pregnancy, drugs.... There is so much to make kids go the wrong way. Nine out of ten kids [her figures] are becoming pregnant while they're still in their teens. I had her [Leila] when I was fifteen and I don't want her do the same thing."

## Keys to a Successful Youth/Young Adult Community Program

1. The involvement of the whole family right from the start.

2. Adult role models.

3. Make it a total program—every day after school, trips, summer activities, music, sports, educational enrichment.

4. Start with pre-schoolers.

5. Value every child, every person.

6. Accept the support of generous friends.

7. Make the achievements of the youth and young adult visible. They will serve as role models for others.

8. Make it fun.

—*Pooled from the staff*

## How You Can Do It—Ten Commandments

1. Go out and meet the kids.

2. Follow them home and get to know their parents.

3. Open the center up and personally invite the community.

4. Accept and love first; correct and judge later. Be patient when people fail and give them another chance...again and again and again.

5. Create standards and reward achievement.

6. Give kids something to reach for.

7. Find a place for everyone.

8. Expect yourself, staff, and volunteers to demonstrate positive attitudes.

9. Be creative and when the system's against you, beat it!

10. Create a community presence.

—*Colenzo Hubbard*

## Quotable Quotes from Colenzo Hubbard

"God was at work in us when we were no larger than a black-eyed pea."

"We're unique to God. Just imagine your fingerprint! No one else in the whole world has your fingerprint. God said, 'I'm going to make you special. I'm going to prove it by giving you a fingerprint no one else has.'"

"If you trust kids, really trust them, they will pretty much die for you."

"Anything they can conceive they can achieve, but first they must believe."

## The Dream Lives on...

So the dream lives on.....Because of the Emmanuel Center kids can dream and some of those dreams are coming true. They can hope and not be disappointed. They can see visions of a better world breaking open just enough to feel the light shining in their lives. It is happening amid two crack-infested public housing projects just as surely as 'Ol Man River just keeps rollin' along. The other King of Memphis, Elvis Presley, King of Rock and Roll, may have lived close by at Graceland, but everyone touched by the brightly shining stars at the Emmanuel Center knows where true amazing grace is to be found.

# Singing for GOD

## SUBURBAN CONGREGATION

Carolyn Hunt was at a loss as to how to help her son, Ryan, feel better about his move from Massachusetts to California. He thought California was "the end of the world." The move was occasioned by the job transfer of Ryan's father, Gary, and Ryan was not happy about it. Then the family had a visit from St. Timothy's youth minister, the Rev. Mark Spaulding, and from that moment on things began to look up. As Carolyn now reflects, "Mark visited and met the family. He asked Ryan if he might have an interest in playing in the rock band just getting off the ground." Ryan did, and, according to Carolyn, "It made an enormous difference. Ryan felt he has a plan. Through Mark, God reached out and it saved us."

Three years ago, Aslan, a rock band composed of teenagers and their youth minister, started playing Christian rock music for the newly established contemporary service at 9:00 on Sunday morning. The band's name, Aslan, is Turkish for "lion," and was taken from the name of a character in C.S. Lewis' *The Chronicles of Narnia*. It now numbers over a dozen junior and senior high schoolers. They compose their own music and lyrics, and they have a touring group, which has played at many loca-

tions around the country. They are about to record their third CD.

The band's motto is "We sing for God," and indeed they do. "It is unlike anything in the world to hear the applause and cheers for God's music," Lizz Parsons, a singer, explains. "'Tell all the World' and 'Give it All Away' get people rockin' and having a good time praising God! One of the greatest joys is to watch three- and four-year-old kids singing along with one of our albums. Those kids will grow up believing that God is 'cool,' thanks to our ministry."

The Aslan sound is a mixture of folk music, classic rock, and pop. It is loud. It is melodic without being soft or sentimental. "Where Have I Seen You," illustrates their realistic yet loving approach to lyrics:

*People are hungry.*
*Waiting in line.*
*We are called to serve.*
*How we spend our time.*
*Prisons are full.*
*People tell me.*
*Too costly to keep.*
*Dispose of all those souls.*
*Where have I seen you?*
*Oh Lord, so many in need to care.*
*How shall I serve you?*
*Share love. Come follow me.*
*Strangers among us.*
*Not welcome here.*
*But for some people,*
*Who stand with open arms,*
*God will call them.*
*Sisters of the soul,*
*And to this faithful:*
*God will make whole.*

The title of their first album, "Give it all Away!" comes from its signature song, the first they ever wrote. It is a fitting one, since all the proceeds of their albums are given away to outreach. Whether in the studio, church, or in concert, members of Aslan feel God's love and healing power in their lives, but they know that if it is going to remain real for them they have to "Give it all Away."

There is Aslan Touring Band and Aslan. Any youth member can come along on a Thursday evening and play with Aslan. The touring group is more intentionally selected and is composed of kids who are willing to spend ten to fifteen hours a week in rehearsal and on the road. This current group of tourers is about to graduate, to begin college, or join the working world, but behind them are those just a little younger who are eager to take their places in concert. Charles Altura, age 12, is one of them. He says, "I'm looking forward to next fall. There's going to be a new band and I'm excited about a new beginning."

Dorie Patterson, parent of C.J., age 10, and Kristen, age 13, worships at 9:00, the fastest growing of St. Timothy's three Sunday services. Sitting in a front row close to the music, Dorie said, "St. Timothy's is a wonderful place that welcomes youth on their own terms and nurtures them. Mark (youth minister and leader of the band who plays acoustic guitar and sings) is a unique person. He is a priest. He has high intellectual ability without all its trappings. He's able to speak the language of music and in doing so he never risks the integrity of the church. He has a solid theological integrity, yet he speaks the same language the kids speak. He bridges the gap."

# DANVILLE, CALIFORNIA

**Community**: Located in Contra Costa County at the foot of Mt. Diablo, east of San Francisco, Danville is an upper middle class, mostly white community of about 34,000.

**Church**: St. Timothy's Episcopal Church: The church was built in 1955 and has been expanding ever since. Over a six-year period it's budget has grown from $200,000 to $600,000. It has a pre-school, Noah's Ark, with its own staff. This summer, Grace House, a handsome $1.77 million additional building will be completed. It will provide a greatly enlarged meeting space for youth and young adults with a comfortable lounge, music room, large multi-purpose room, and kitchen facilities.

St. Timothy's has 1,275 members, 347 pledging units. There are three full-time clergy and several part-timers.

## Who Makes It Happen? Introducing A Few Members of Aslan

**Sean Potts**, age 19, plays bass guitar, melody and harmony vocals.

*Nobody in Aslan will "harsh your gig." It doesn't matter who you are. We make it a point to be inclusive, and I take Aslan's sense of inclusivity wherever I go. At its best, Aslan is the kind of community I want to live in the rest of my life. Sure, there've been times when we haven't gotten along, but on the whole, Aslan means caring for and loving each other unconditionally.*

**Ryan Hunt**, age 18, plays lead guitar.

*I'd just moved to California and went to a really bad school. One day Mark came over and said "I heard you play guitar," and asked me if I wanted to be in the band.*

**Katie Parsons**, age 17, sings harmony.

*Singing in the band has given me more confidence. After a concert someone came up to me and said, "Your voice really carried well." No one ever said that to me before.*

**Kevin Soult**, age 17, plays drums.

*At first I started playing the guitar, left-handed guitar. Then a year-and-a-half into it, my guitar broke. Neck broke right off of it. I was miserable but then I started playing the drums. I took lessons for about ten months and it's been great.*

**Jennifer Ketcham**, age 13, sings harmony.

*I think that the reason that Aslan is what it is now is because it's our way to God. Not through prayers but through our voices and our instruments.*

**Michael Kuhlmann**, age 16, is the sound engineer and also plays bass guitar.

*Aslan means a lot to me, both practicing and playing with the group. What I like best is that we're all equals, regardless of our ages.*

Other Aslan members include: Susan Strane, age 16; and Lizz Parsons, age 19, who are singers. Charles Altura, age 12, plays keyboard; and Jennifer Hornbeck, age 19, is Aslan's manager.

### How to Start a Band—Some Pointers from Aslan's Members

1. Start small. Start very casually. Begin with a guitar and a tambourine. You do not need a sound system at first.

2. Find a leader who is musically adept and can talk to people. Look for an adult member of the church who can give you the time and start to move things for you.

3. You do not need any special talent to join a band. You need desire.

4. Build interest and impress the clergy. As they gain confidence in you, they will help you get started.

5. You need a willing parish that will help with financial support. As you get going, you will need a sound system and more instruments.

### YOUTH MINISTRY—Tree of Life

Aslan is just the most visible of St. Timothy's youth programs. There is a wide range of other activities and programs going on every day and most nights of the week. Some are introductory, just fun, and require no commitment beyond the specific activity. Others require time and the risk of revealing one's self.

The Tree of Life is our pictorial metaphor for all we have going on here at Saint Timothy's youth ministry.

We call it the Tree of Life because we believe that the programs we have to offer are indeed the life-giving ministry of Jesus Christ. We realize that ONE program is NOT going to meet the needs of all teenagers in this valley, therefore we offer the following to choose from. Take a look at the programs below, see what interests you and dive in. Hint: start with the programs closest to the trunk of the tree and as you feel more comfortable, climb on up to another branch.

- **Drop-in Center**. Drop in to Grace House to listen to music, watch movies, hang out with friends, play pool, eat, whatever. This is YOUR center. Come down anytime and enjoy it!

- **Mystery Nights**. Designed for a small group of people (six or less). Join an advisor at the church at 6:00 pm and bring $7. Then be prepared for a meal and an evening of fun. What do you do? That's the mystery!

- **Breakfast Club**. Come together to begin the day (6:15-7:00 am) to share God's Word over muffins and oj in Mark's living room.

- **B and B**. Burger King and Bible meets every Thursday afternoon. We meet at the church at 4:30 and then head for BK to grab a bite and talk about current events in our lives and the Bible connection.

# Movie Nights

A night at the movies is good for everyone! And there are some GREAT movies out this summer! Come on down and we will decide on the evening which movie we are going to see (for a mixed Jr & Sr high group count on a PG movie.)

Grab some popcorn and get ready to share a movie with some [...]

## Bikes

### MOUNTAIN MANIA

Last summer we decided to get Mark exercising with us. Everyone had a great time riding around town and stopping in to see friends on the way.

We had such great feedback that we've decided to do it again this summer.

So grab your bike, or blades, and come on down this summer and join us for a warm summer evening.

## Youth Ministry Kick off!

*by a ghost advisor writer*

Hey, Hey, Hey, all you wacky teenagers out there! It's time again for another year of smokin' youth events here at St. Tim's. And we're gonna kick it off this year with the annual Progressive Dinner. The dinner will include a bicycle tour to different houses of the parish while eating a different course of our meal along the way. At the end of the ride we will get cooled off with ice cream sundaes and swimming. So if your down for a bike ride, some [...]ning, some good food, and some good friends we'll see you on Saturday the 16th. [...]nior and Senior highers are invited and don't forget to BRING A FRIEND. The [...] of the event is $5. If you don't want to ride your bike we'll also have a car driving [...] house to house. Since this event is on a Saturday night we also may go out after as [...] a couple extra bucks if you want. So bring your bike, your swim suit, and come [...] to have fun at the Progressive Dinner.

Saint Timothy's Youth Ministry

## The Next Generation

- **Follow Me**. From soup kitchens to collecting clothes, this group wants to reach out! Follow Me meets on the second Sunday of every month from 4-6 pm.

- **Sunday Nite Live**. Programs for Sunday Nite Live are designed to attend to the needs and concerns of teens in the valley. If you are wondering about something, need a place to talk or meet new friends, Live is a GREAT place to begin.

- **Social Action Lock-ins**. This is a 30-hour retreat designed to bring an awareness of the world around us home. Not only do we have a lot of fun but we learn about some of the people who hurt in this big world of ours, and are empowered to DO something about it.

- **Movie Nights**. Come on down and we will decide on the evening which movie we are going to see. Grab some popcorn and get ready to share a movie with some friends! See calendar for dates.

- **Bikes/Mountain Mania**. Everyone has a great time riding around town and stopping in to see friends on the way. So grab your bike or blades and come on down. Check calendar for dates.

- **Dead Theologians Society**. "Dead Theo's" is modeled after the movie, Dead Poet's Society, but instead of looking at poets of antiquity to help make sense of today's world, the group looks at Scripture and theologians of antiquity to help make sense of everyday life. Meets Sunday morning. All high school teens welcome!

- **Progressive Dinner and Dive-in Movie**. The meal includes several different courses that will be eaten at various houses the group will bike or ride to on the way to our dessert and dive-in movie. What is a dive-in movie? Watching a movie while in or near the pool, probably "Jaws" or "the Beast."

- **Day Trips**. From time to time throughout the year, youth ministry sponsors trips to all kinds of places. In the summer it might be to Great America, an amusement park, or to water slides. This is a perfect opportunity to invite your friends and introduce them to members of the community.

- **Snow Retreats**. We see who has a mountain house and use it for a weekend retreat for high school kids.

- **Summer Work Camp**. Summer Work Camp is an opportunity to go into another community and help the residents by doing light construction and renovations. Work camps go to Navajoland and Mexico.

- **Theme Parties**. Sometimes these parties take place at holiday seasons like Christmas or anytime with a banana night or water Olympics.

- **The Next Generation**. This is our youth newspaper. *The Next Generation* staff meets on the third Sunday of the month to write, design, and lay out the paper. If you desire the *power of the pen*, then this is the group for you.

- **838-STYM**. Youth ministry information line. Open 24 hours, 7 days a week. Call anytime to find out about or reserve a spot on the latest youth ministry events.

- **Have a Question**? Just need to talk? We are available anytime. Just pick up the phone and "reach out and touch someone." [The names and telephone numbers of 20 contacts are listed in the flier.]

## Who Makes It Happen? The Youth Ministers.

The youth ministers are ten adults and eight teenagers working with the youth minister, the Rev. Mark Spaulding, a specialist in youth ministry. Together they design, implement, and evaluate all youth ministry programs. Teams of three advisors, working on a four-five week rotation, plan Sunday Nite Live. As the weeks of the month progress, the programs become more intensive. Thus, a good time to introduce newcomers is during the first or second week.

An indication of the trust the church puts in its youth ministers is demonstrated by the fact that each one has a key to the church. They do not take this responsibility lightly.

### QUOTABLE QUOTES FROM MARK SPAULDING

"Everytime I see a kid, whether in the streets, in the supermarket, anyplace, I try to find out how I can get him or her to call this place (St. Timothy's) home. I want St. Timothy's to be an oasis in this valley."

"I don't get paid to go to theme parks!! If I never saw another one in my life, I'd be a happy guy. I do it as a tool to build on. I use it as a doorway, a conduit, to what's meaningful and important."

"Everything I do is to create communities of a saving faith belief system based on love, honesty, integrity. That's all I do for a living."

"I have a personal goal to get every kid to go on a work camp at least once." Why? "Being what this place is (largely white and upper middle class), I know that the majority of St. Timothy's kids will come into positions of power and influence. To do so responsibly they need to have seen the other side. My soul was indelibly marked by India and the Philippines."

## Work Camp

Lizz Parsons, age 19, a student at Diablo Community College said:

> I went to Gallup, New Mexico on a one-week work camp. We flew into Albuquerque and stayed at a school in Gallup. Every morning we drove about 45 minutes to the Navajo Reservation. My "Resident" had a little three-room house half-built. Money had run out so he hadn't been able to finish it. We built stairs, drywalled inside, layered stucco on the outside and refinished the walls.

> "Grandpa" was 96-years-old and blind. He spoke only Navajo. His grandson, Asa, a 16-year-old, translated for us. Members of his family lived in other houses around his. In addition to Grandpa's family, I worked with six other members of the group who had come from Texas, Connecticut, Delaware, and Ohio. We'd never met before so we all learned a lot about communicating.

> On the last day after we'd finished, Grandpa was sitting on a couch under the tree. We told him we were done and he looked at us and said, "Thank you." Asa told us that he had been practicing all week to say it. That was his gift to us. That was what

*he could give. It was very humbling. Everyone was crying. It only took a minute but I'll never forget it.*

*What did I learn from the experience? It was 120 degrees in the shade, but it was more than worth it. It's getting down and dirty. It's a matter of survival. It's a sobering experience. It made me realize how lucky we are to have a roof over our heads and a refrigerator. The experience put me in touch with myself and of all I can and ought to do.*

*I was equally touched by Sean Potts' experience. He was working on another house and at the end of the week his "Resident" walked out to the kids carrying a tray full of silver and turquoise jewelry, and he said "You just help yourself and pick out something you want." I just couldn't believe it. The man had nothing but he was offering to the kids the best of what he had, his precious treasures.*

*What else can I say? Going to a work camp changes you.*

## Potatoes

Last Sunday I exploded a potato thing that I was cooking in the oven. As I watched it explode, it got me thinking about life. Now, you're probably thinking, "boy is this girl crazy," but I'm serious, those potatoes were a lot like life.

You never know when something in your life, or in a loved one's life, is going to explode. You could be cruising right along, and then kaboom, everything sane in your life is blown to bits. Sometimes you have to watch it happen and then clean up as much of the mess as you can later.

Sometimes, if you get too much going on in your life, the stress takes over another part of your life, like your family, friends, or schoolwork, and that explodes as well. This all goes to show that people just have to pay attention to the "temperature" of their ovens.

—Susan Strane, age 16

*First published in* The Next Generation, *St. Timothy's youth newsletter.*

## Ten Commandments for a Successful Youth Program

1. The ordained staff must have a high commitment to children and youth. This is far easier to say than live!

2. The parish community must be committed to children and youth. Adultism will kill any youth program. Commitment is more attitude than money. Youth must be seen, heard, respected, and appreciated as they are, who they are.

3. The youth minister must be committed, creative, willing to listen, model high ethical behavior, and have and enforce clear boundaries and expectations.

4. The youth program must be as broad as possible. The more opportunities there are, the more probable that individual youth will be attracted. Examples include: youth music (choirs, bands, jam sessions), "youth groups," retreats, fun stuff (lock-ins/overnights), family services (where youth participate, where music speaks to the youth, etc.).

5. The program must be connected to the community (town, schools) and the youth of the community. Otherwise the program is out of context and disconnected.

6. Have fun.

7. Pick youth advisors carefully. We all know the kinds of parents who have neither the patience, flexibility, nor savvy to roll with a youth program. It's also important that youth advisors can serve as appropriate role models for our youth. Youth advisors must be fearless about and willing to examine their own stuff (biases, past, etc.). Youth advisors must be willing to be wrong and know they do not know it all.

8. Remember, we are theologically based. Youth want to hear about God and how God impacts on their lives.

9. The programs must be relevant. Be willing to talk and listen about drugs, sex, suicide, divorce, other religions, etc. Youth ministry is not for the faint of heart.

10. Be quiet and listen to God, youth, and your own heart.

—John Potts, *father of Sean and Katie*

## Accepting the Challenge

The members of St. Timothy's have accepted the challenge. They have given youth ministry the highest priority, one that they have backed up with time, money, and staff. More importantly, they have created a space, both material space and space in terms of an open, positive attitude, to allow youth ministry to grow, develop, and flower.

According to the Right Reverend William Swing, bishop of California,

We in this diocese give youth and young adult ministry our highest attention. Our first priority is our commitment. Secondly, we stress the development of youth ministry and training. We give prominence to our youth leaders.

It's most important to create a vacuum so that kids can come in and fill it. The adults have to do this. They have to open up the churches. In addition you have to have the view that ministry to and with youth is not just a lark, a "nice thing to do." It's a matter of life and death. If you don't understand its urgency, you'll treat it casually. When youth are genuinely valued, it makes all the difference in the world.

Maureen Horton, from St. Paul's Church, Walnut Creek, interviewed while attending an Aslan concert, captured both the need and the challenge of youth ministry:

Kids need a vehicle to be included. Sunday morning doesn't do it. This parish has created a safe environment. It has made a commitment to the kids, which it backs up with space and money. It has Mark who really gets down with the kids.

The kids are here to challenge the church. The church has to decide whether it wants to be challenged....And challenge means change.

# The Shadowlands of Main Street, Hometown, USA

## SUBURBAN COMMUNITY OUTREACH

Marshfield, Massachusetts is an ordinary New England coastal town with a population of somewhere between 25,000 and 30,000. Entering Marshfield along a secondary road from Boston, one notices the marshy fields of eel grass with little rivulets running through it, and the scent in the air of the sea beyond. The road winds its way to the water's edge at Ocean Bluff and Brant Rock where summer is just beginning, as seasonal residents remove windblown wooden shutters from their cottages. Marshfield has other enclaves—Marshfield Hills, North Marshfield, Fieldston. These are inland and nestled amid rolling hills and twisting streets.

The visitor sees the small cottages built closely together, interspersed with more solid year-round homes in Marshfield's coastal neighborhoods. In "The Hills" one observes large lots with bigger houses, more glass, larger garages, landscaped yards, punctuated by a few classic New England, colonial clapboards. But it would take a local resident to feel the subtle distinctions of class and culture among the areas of Marshfield. Marshfield is overwhelmingly white and Roman Catholic. Marshfield's only racial problem is that it has no appreciable numbers of anyone other than white Americans. Its residents are neither very rich nor very poor. While some of its residents are struggling economically, Marshfield has no pockets of extreme poverty. Its schools are neither the best nor the worst in the Commonwealth of Massachusetts. When one thinks of a typical American town anywhere, one imagines a Marshfield—Main Street, Hometown USA. And we had better sit up and listen carefully to a representative group of young adults as they tell us about life in the shadowlands, the shadowlands of towns just like Marshfield all over the USA.

What follows is a story about a priest with a compassionate heart, a head for justice, and the tools of a social scientist, who decided to enter the world of the shadowlands, get to know the youth and young adults, listen to them carefully and, with them, visualize what the church could do to respond to what they tell him.

The Rev. Charles Virga, known universally as Charlie, is priest-in-charge of Trinity Church, Marshfield Hills. This is a congregation that supports Charlie's work with young people both in and beyond the parish. The support of the parish is crucial to Charlie's success.

Charlie and his family live in Brant Rock. They moved there intentionally because this is where most of the young people he deals with in his ministry live. He has developed a model for youth/young adult ministry using social analysis theory.

## How Do We Reach the Young Adult Age Group?

*According to Charlie:*

I've had a rising level of frustration about the question we always seem to be asking in the Episcopal Church, which is—how do we reach the young adult age group? We do a pretty good job for children in their younger years, but when they grow up there's nothing for them to do and we don't know what to do.

Then I started to realize that it's an adult need and an adult question.

Young adults need space to stay away, while at the same time some ways to stay connected. Marshfield is full of young adults who have no connection with the social structures in the community.

*[Turning to Gus, the co-leader of the weekend]* No matter what *you* do, you have a back-up system. Lots of these young people have no first or second back-up. They are third world kids trapped in a first world view.

You have to go to the margins of the community and ask the questions. If you address the margins, you'll catch everyone in  between.

**The Plan:** Charlie invited a group of eight "unchurched" young adults to attend an overnight retreat to serve as a focus group to consider the question of how Trinity Church could respond to the needs of young adults in Marshfield. We met at an inn in Rockport from Friday evening until Saturday afternoon. Gus Jacobson, a 25-year-old school teacher, helped in the leadership of the retreat.

Friday night was spent with introductions and ice-breaking exercises. On Saturday Charlie engaged the group in a process of social analysis.

**The Group:**

Michael Snyder, age 21. "I'm working but I'm thinking about going back to school."

Tracy Clements, age 23. "I'm working. I would like to be successful in life."

Eric Petrosevich, age 18. "I just graduated from high school and I'm looking for a job."

Jon McDormand, age 18. "I graduated from high school and I'm working."

Kristen Dowd, age 20. "I'm a full-time nanny now, but in the fall I'll go back to Massasoit Community College."

Stacey McDormand, 21. "I'm working, hoping to be happy and successful."

Peter Breen, age 20. "I'll be a senior at Holy Cross College. This summer I'm working."

David Howes, age 22. "I'm working full-time and going to school at Bridgewater State College. I plan to get a master's in criminology. I'd like to become a cop."

**Identification of the Issues:** The group was divided into three sections to discuss: What are the structures in the community that help and hinder youth/young adults?

## Structures that hinder: Concerns/problems (In their words):

### LIST A

- Substance abuse.

- Pregnancies and STDs (sexually transmitted diseases). People are using nothing to protect themselves and they don't care.

- Drunk driving.

- Lack of education. Kids are dropping out of school and no one cares.

- Violence—domestic and family abuse. Parents abuse their kids physically and mentally.

- Broken homes. People don't care about their kids. Drugs come before their kids. This is a big problem in Marshfield. Mothers show up at the daycare center to pick up their kids, high, and drunk.

- Boredom. Kids our age don't have jobs. They aren't going to school. They just sit around. They have no motivation. Alcohol and drugs play a large part in this and this is related to violence.

- Future—concerns for what they're going to do for the rest of their lives.

**Positive Structures:**
- Charlie Virga
- Parents and family
- School/Teachers (particular teachers)
- Friends
- Church
- College
- Youth groups

## Think of all the words that come to mind when you hear the word "church."

**List B**

- Religion
- God
- Priest
- Community
- Calmness
- Songs
- Helpful

- Responsibility
- Good
- Tradition
- Bonding
- Bible
- Forgiveness

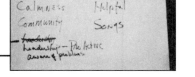

Tracy, "I say 'calmness' because if I've been stressed out I leave the church feeling calm and relaxed."

David, "It's a feeling of relief when I go to church. All my problems—I leave them right at the door. Church helps you find the good in any bad situation. It helps turn problems into positives."

Kristen, "I feel free. I leave my problems behind. I feel God's forgiveness and he helps me."

Jon, "At work everyone's pissed off. I get pissed off. You go to church to be forgiven."

## Then why don't young adults go to church?

Kristen, "They have better things to do. It just doesn't click with them. It's very serious. You gotta listen to the priest, and you can't understand what he's saying. You can't hear because he's just mumbling. My church is very boring."

Jon, "You don't have to go to church to feel forgiven."

## There's a large gap between the concerns and problems and church. What needs to happen for List B to address List A?

Tracy, "The church would have to take more responsibility. If I were pregnant the **last place** I'd go to for help would be the church. Maybe if the church were more forgiving instead of judging....Maybe if people in the church were just kind and looked for ways to help out young adults."

Stacey, "The church would have to act as if they sympathized."

David, "You could have church counselors just like they have in school. The church really ought to be more pro-active rather than re-active. They ought to become aware of what the problems are out there."

## Social Analysis

Social analysis is an understanding of the interrelationships between one's own life experience with society and history. It enables us to make linkages between our personal stories and the socio-political context of which these stories are a part.

1. Social analysis develops a framework for understanding the distribution of power and the access to wealth, goods, and services that accompany power. They recognize that in our present hierarchical system (churches, schools, corporations) persons are assigned positions of domination and subordination primarily on the basis of class, race or ethnicity, gender, age, and geography.

2. Social analysis continually asks questions about problems, events, issues, and structures that affect people's lives. Within this framework for doing social analysis, we ask such questions as: Who makes the decisions? Who benefits from the decisions? What structures support this situation? What symbols make it appear "right"?

3. Social analysis recognizes that even as we arrive at partial answers, new questions are being generated. It asks: What do we know as fact? What are our hunches? What additional information do we need and where can we get it?

4. Social analysis seeks out available sources of information. It does so with a healthy suspicion of the tactics of misinformation, and misinformation used by those interested in preserving the status quo.

5. Understanding the linkages of all issues and causes, social analysis continually deepens the analysis in order to comprehend our particular concern as multi-leveled and interconnected. In social analysis we challenge ourselves to broaden our analysis and to think globally as members of a world society.

— Charles Virga

*Adapted from the Emmanuel College Urban Parish Program.*

GLOBAL

COMMUNITY

PERSONAL

## The Social Analysis Bull's Eye as Applied to Young Adults in Marshfield:

Charlie gives each participant a social analysis bulls eye. He asks them to write their names in the center and then to chart the organizations, groups, forces, persons, etc. that influence their lives and to place them under their appropriate spheres of influence: personal, community, and global.

Eric volunteers to share his bull's eye. He lists: gas station, home, job, family, Marshfield, school, police, stores, friends, park. These are mostly centered within the first and second rings—personal and community. Jon and Tracy follow in a similar manner.

Charlie then asks them to take everything on the list and individually indicate whether they are positive, negative, or neutral.

Family, friends, church, and jobs were generally perceived as positive; police and school as negative; stores, the gas station, the park as neutral.

Looking at the completed bull's eyes, each participant was able to determine if the forces of influence in his/her life were primarily positive, negative, or neutral.

## The following questions were asked:

- If you could change one negative into a positive, what would it be and how would your life be changed?

[Eric indicated that for him it would be the police. "If they'd be off my butt, I wouldn't always be in the wrong place at the wrong time!"]

- Who has the potential to help? [Family, friends, church.] It is pointed out that the people and organizations with the most potential to help are those furthest to the edge of the list—schools, church, government.

## A Typical Young Adult Who Lives in Marshfield

1. Charlie then directs the attention of the group to List A, "Structures that Hinder: Concerns/Problems," and asks them if they have friends who are affected by any of those issues/concerns. [They all nod affirmatively.]

2. The group is split into half and the participants are directed to: Tell a story of someone from List A.

Story 1: The parents arrive high or drunk at the pre-school to pick up their child. They are smoking pot four or five times daily. When you are drunk you may have unsafe sex, which could lead to pregnancy.

Story 2: The story centers around a young adult male whose parents are divorced. He cannot get along with his stepfather. He gets depressed about it and turns to drugs. This is expensive and he has to steal to support his habit. Frustrated and angry, he starts beating his girlfriend, thus abusing the only support he has.

3. Do you know these people? [Again, they all nod affirmatively.] Their stories are charted on the bull's eye.

4. What is missing from their lives? The group then lists: church, school, work, loving family, friends.

## The Church's Response

The earlier phrase/question is repeated and re-stated: There is a large gap between the concerns and problems of young adults in Marshfield, and the church. **What would a concrete response be on the part of the church?**

- The church should not be afraid to go to the power structures and advocate for the well-being of kids

- The church could offer someone to talk to (counseling and acceptance).

- The church could offer vocational counseling.

- The church could sponsor recreational teams and leagues.

- They could develop sports facilities.

- The church could become a gathering place.

- Parent education classes. "Parents are way too lenient with their children. They're drinking and doing drugs. I wish the church could help them. It may be too late for our parents, but the church should help parents of kids coming along behind us. If the parents are helped, so will the kids be helped." —Mike [All nod in agreement.]

> Social analysis needs to be integrated into every aspect of our youth ministry, from the Sunday night youth meeting to our social action projects. Our failure to do so is to allow our work with youth to remain complicit with the structures that oppress the very youth we are committed to helping.
>
> —Charles Virga

## Light in the Shadowlands

The group members are feeling tired but satisfied. They are trying to decide whether to dive into the pool for one last swim, or to just drive home to Marshfield. It is a day-and-a-half later and the weekend has ended. They are all smiling. They are laughing a little more readily than when the weekend began. Now they are holding their heads higher. They cannot remember when the last time was that someone asked them about what is going on in their lives and in the lives of others like them in Marshfield. There may be a way to go to translate the needs of Marshfield's young adults into programs, but for now, a light has been switched on in the shadowlands.

## As a result of the gathering:

- Twelve young people attended the Episcopal Youth Event in Indiana.

- A residence for homeless youth is being established in the community.

- A Community Drop-in Center is in the planning. Recreation, a job placement service, and legal advocacy programs will be provided.

- Trinity Church is seen as a place that hears the voices of young people and their concerns.

# Opening Doors, Building Connections

## URBAN CONGREGATION

"The Chinese always do things through connections," according to Jimmy Cheng, a young adult member of Church of Our Savior. "I never heard of a guy who just went by a church, saw the sign, and went in. I first came with my brother, Tommy. He'd come because a friend invited him." Jimmy came to New York six years ago from Hong Kong with his parents and brother. Now 18 years old, he is a computer science major at Pace College.

Louis Leung is 20. Also a student at Pace, he has been in the USA for five years. "Jimmy is the first person I got to know when I came to the USA. He lives near me in Brooklyn. We met in the summer school program. He helped me out. He understood how it was not to be able to say one word in English."

All of the ministries of Church of Our Savior are about opening doors and building connections. They are about welcoming those who come as strangers and making them friends.

Since 1965 when the USA, recognizing its bias in favor of European countries, overhauled its immigration laws, Chinese immigrants from all over the world have been arriving in ever-increasing numbers. About 20,000 Chinese each year legally immigrate from China and 6,000 from Hong Kong. Approximately 17 percent of the total settle in New York City, giving New York's Chinatown the largest urban Chinese population in the country, surpassing even San Francisco's. New York's Chinatown covers about a five-mile radius and includes some 200,000 people. Chinese owned businesses abound and there are at least four daily, New York Chinese newspapers.

When Church of Our Savior was consecrated in 1992 it was New York's first new Episcopal church in thirty years. Its original tenement buildings were the first home of the famed Henry Street Settlement House, and later became the site of St. Christopher's Chapel, a mission of Trinity Church, Wall Street. The three old tenement houses were torn down and replaced by a handsome 12-story, 32-unit residential condominium with beautiful, modern church offices, classrooms, a gym, and a community center. The church has 150 families. They come from China, Taiwan, Hong Kong,

Singapore and Malaysia. About 5 percent are American born; 70 percent commute in from the suburbs to attend Our Savior. The church is overseen by a lay administrator with a collegial style, Mr. Peter Ng, and a vestry, whose members are mostly under forty.

While the church has an active youth/young adult program, Vineyard Fellowship, similar to any parish's youth fellowship, Our Savior is unique in that virtually all its ministries are designed to serve the newly arrived, young adult population.

What do the newly arrived need to get started? Language, skills, and jobs. Our Savior is committed to filling those basic needs. There are classes in English as a second language, citizenship classes, computer camp, job training, counseling, and a computer repair and distribution program. The church has its own cottage industry, a desktop publishing industry called Mission Graphics. It sponsors joint programs with the City of New York and its board of education. Chinatown Manpower Project, Inc., utilizes church facilities and benefits church members. Our Savior combines entrepreneurial talent with ministry. The church needs the financial support outside contracts supply, and its newly arrived members need the opportunities that the organizations can provide. The church also hosts games and sporting events, and most recently, seeing Chinatown children's need to make beautiful music, they instituted the Jubilee Youth Chorale, which has forty choristers and is growing.

## The Ministries of Church of Our Savior:

- **English Classes.** Every Sunday morning at 10 am we have three levels of free English classes to teach reading, writing, and phrases that will help you communicate better in the United States. Take these classes and feel more confident when you visit the doctor, the post office, or the bank.

- **Mission Graphics.** Our Savior services nonprofit organizations in the design and printing of materials such as brochures, flyers, business cards, books, etc. We feel that nonprofit organizations should not produce materials inferior to corporate America simply because of lack of sufficient funds. We are currently working on a joint project with the Diocese of Taiwan on a Chinese Book of Common Prayer.

- **Computer Summer Camp.** For youth from ages six to fifteen. Lessons are held every Saturday.

- **Chinatown Manpower Project, Inc.** Offers training in office management, interpersonal skills, time management, accounting, computer software application, and job counseling and placement.

- **Jubilee Youth Chorale.** For young choristers to come to know Western and Chinese music and for the pleasure and discipline that comes from corporate music-making. Weekly rehearsals are rigorous because we have the unequivocal conviction that only the fruits of diligence can be genuinely interesting and edifying.

歌聲處處揚
Sound of Music
Tan Yue Chorale & Jubilee Youth Chorale
談樂合唱團與金禧青少年合唱團
In Concert
演唱會

- **Tutorial Program.** Help in all subjects to school children.
- **Health Fairs.** In cooperation with St. Vincent's Medical Center and supported by local banks and businesses, the church sponsors health fairs once a year. Includes workshops, flu shots, glucose testing, breast cancer screening, eye and ear tests, dental exams, and lectures from doctors. "Jesus healed not only people's souls but their bodies also."
- **Weddings.** The chapel of Our Savior is open to all who wish to be joined in marriage blessed by God. The parish will also arrange for wedding receptions.
- **Vineyard Youth Fellowship.** The fellowship coordinates most of the programs and its members serve as teachers. See separate article on the Vineyard Youth Fellowship.

## How are these programs evangelistic?

The mission of the parish is to reach out to the community and meet its needs.

According to Pamela Tang:

*First we bring people in for what they need; then we evangelize. Our philosophy is simple. People want to serve the community, meet its needs, and are using the church to do that. Something like the Youth Chorale is good for us. The congregation can take ownership and be energized by the fact that others can use the church. We can see new opportunities in others, reaching out and the community reaching in. It creates networks with the world, and we are all blessed.*

### Hub of the Community

We believe that the church should be the spiritual, artistic, and educational hub of the community; it is a sanctuary for all, not a castle to fend off outsiders. Therefore we aim to empower our community by offering programs and services....

—Wardens George Man, Pamela Tang and Peter Ng, Parish Administrator

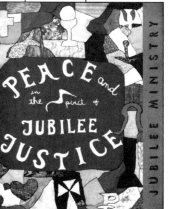

## Profile of the Vineyard Youth Fellowship

"I am the vine, you are the branches. Those who abide in me and I in them bear much fruit...." —John 15: 5

Vineyard Fellowship is a bilingual Christian fellowship. Spiritual songs are sung in both languages. Bible study, topical workshops, and group sharing are conducted in Cantonese and English in small groups. Composed mainly of teenagers and young adults, Vineyard Fellowship hosts attractive programs varying from the leisurely and fun to the serious and challenging.

The objective of Vineyard Fellowship is twofold: witnessing to nonbelievers and nurturing young Christians. Identifying a particular Sunday as "Bring-a-Friend Day" and encouraging members to pray for and bring their friends on that Sunday is one way we seek to evangelize the unchurched. Skits and personal testimonies are usually planned on those Sundays to introduce newcomers to the good news of the gospel. We also attempt to help our members grow in biblical knowledge, faith, and love.

As our Vineyard motto says, "Don't let anyone look down on you because you are young, but set an example to the believers in speech, in life, in love, in faith, and in purity" (1 Tim. 4:12). Without doubt, much attention is paid to Bible studies and topical workshops to stimulate members' desire for God's Word. Vineyard also hosts Bible Jeopardy and Bible Pictionary.

Vineyard Fellowship meets every Sunday from 9—10 am for singspiration, learning, and prayer, but there are lots of activities that take place at other times. Picnics, ice-skating parties, graduation dinners, ball games, and family fellowship (we simply pick someone's house and run a fellowship meeting there), are regularly scheduled to promote unity among members. As members of the body of Christ, we strongly believe that we are one big family and we "...should look not only to our own interests, but also to the interests of others" (Phil. 2:4).

—Members of Vineyard Fellowship

## Who Makes It Happen?

Introducing Some of the Leaders:

**Yvonne Chan**, age 23, is co-leader of the Vineyard Fellowship. Yvonne came to the USA six years ago from Hong Kong. A 1995 graduate of Barnard College, she works as a credit analyst for the Republic National Bank.

Yvonne says:

*Our new church symbolizes new hopes and expectations. Evangelism—the spreading of the good news of our Lord—has and will continue to be one of our main objectives. Learning to love others, although it may seem easy, is not the case if you have to put it into practice. Take a look at the world we are living in. Isn't it full of violence, jealousy, prejudice, and hatred? Conducting services in the heart of Chinatown, we try to bring more people around the area to believe in the teachings of Jesus. Constituted mainly of immigrant families, we are concerned that everyone have a sense of belonging and acceptance in the church.*

*We have grown from a shabby-looking building to the grand church that now stands on Henry Street. Just as in the parable Jesus used to describe the Kingdom of God, it takes a mustard seed, the smallest in the world to become the biggest of all plants. It puts out such large branches that the birds come and make their nests in its shade (Mk. 4:30-32). I don't dare say the Church of Our Savior is the biggest of all plants, but I am sure it is large enough to welcome you.*

**Stephen Chan**, age 22, shares the leadership of Vineyard Fellowship with his sister, Yvonne. Stephen came from Hong Kong six years ago. He graduated from Columbia University in 1996 with a B.S. in chemical engineering. He works as a computer software developer.

*I translate the sermon every Sunday from English into Cantonese for those who don't understand English. When I was on the Columbia University campus, I was active in the Christian group and I did a lot of outreach activities.*

*God's plan for my life? I feel he's calling me to be in more frontline ministry, possibly going to seminary and becoming a pastor. Right now I'm thinking and praying about this.*

*Role models in my life? Other than Jesus?!*

**Pamela Tang**, age 28, is the junior warden of Church of Our Savior. Married to Edison, she lives in Brooklyn and works as administrative assistant to the publisher of the Church Hymnal Corporation.

*My life would be drastically different if I didn't go here. Through the Youth Fellowship I learned leadership skills. I became Peter Ng and Father To's assistant. I worked in the financial aid office at Barnard College, a job that Mrs. To got me. I helped Sheryl Kujawa with the national Episcopal Youth Events, and then Sheryl recommended me for a job at the Episcopal Church Center. From there I went to the Church Hymnal Corporation.*

*All my friends' parents are passing away. I feel fortunate. I can feel God's presence in my life—my parents are alive and my sisters are still here. To me, knowing that there are no major catastrophes is proof that God is in my life. When I was going with my boyfriend, I prayed that he would come to believe in Christ and that he would be baptized. He was and we got married.*

## Introducing a few youth/young adult members...

and what they say about them selves and their lives:

**Wendy Chan**, age 18, is a chemistry major at the University of Chicago.

*I came with my older sister and I grew up here. By the time I grew into my teens I came on my own accord because I wanted to know God and to strengthen my Christianity.*

*I'm going to be a doctor. I like science and discovering new things. In medicine you're always learning. I think the discoveries people make every day are fascinating. I'm lucky because science was always my best subject in school, so it all fits together and works for me.*

**Louie Leung**, age 20, came from Hong Kong five years ago. Louie is now a computer science major at Pace University.

*When I first came to the USA it was very scary. I didn't know anybody. I just sat in the corner. I couldn't say anything. Then I met Jimmy and he made me talk. He asked me questions and he kept it up. I felt like I was in the middle. I had cousins, American cousins, but they could only speak the most basic Cantonese, and then there was school and that was hard too. After awhile, I relaxed a little. I met Jimmy in the summer school program. I started going to the youth group with him. I was the only one who didn't know anybody but the members were very open. They asked me "How's it going?" They worked hard to let me know that Youth Fellowship is a family.*

*Now I admit it! I'd never prayed before, even if I had a problem. I just wanted to pass and get good grades. Then things changed. I started wanting to know why Jesus came here to earth. I wanted to know what Jesus does. Now I want to talk to God and I want him to help me out.*

*Role models, heroes? Stephen (Vineyard Fellowship co-leader). He is kind. He is smart. He has a strong personality. He never thinks, "I'm the brightest, you people are under me." He's very open and friendly. He is never angry. He has the most wonderful character.*

**Jimmy Cheng**, age 18, came from Hong Kong six years ago. Jimmy is a computer science major at Pace University.

*My brother, Tommy, brought me here. It's connections, the Chinese way, one to one. I came with my brother. Someone else had brought him. I brought Louis.*

*We came to this church. We found it beautiful. In Chinatown everything is too old and no one will come to someplace that's old and broken down. But this church is new. It has air conditioning. It attracted us to come here.*

*The members of the fellowship taught me about God. When I was in Hong Kong, I went to a Christian school. They had knowledge, but they didn't teach me anything about the living God. I didn't know who or what God was actually, but here I got a feeling for God in my heart.*

*We all trust in God. That's what brings us together.*

**Simon Chen**, age 18, came with his parents from China to the USA three years ago. Simon just graduated from high school and will soon be a freshman at Brooklyn College. He is an only child because of China's one-child law. In China, he had been recognized as an outstanding badminton player and sent to a special sports training school when he was eleven years old.

*When I first came I went to summer school to learn English. I couldn't even fill out the registration form, that's how bad it was. It took one year to begin feeling comfortable with the language.*

*There are many gangs in my high school, but I study. I concentrate on my work. If you don't get involved with them, they won't bother you.*

*I first came to Our Savior for the English classes that are held on Sunday mornings. After about three weeks, George told me about the 11:00 service, so I went and then I met Stephen and Yvonne and started going to the Fellowship. I liked the games, songs, and Bible study. I'd never been in a church before and my parents were against it. I got baptized last year, and although my mother went to the service, they didn't support it.*

*My parents brought me here to the USA to study, not to go to church! Church takes time. It's not only church, anything that gets in the way of studying is a problem for them. We understand that we have a role to take care of our parents in their old age, so the more successful we are, the more money we make, the better we are able to support them. We respect our elders. We respect those who know more than we do and have more experience, but we feel the pressure.*

*I miss my grandparents, my other relations, my badminton coach. I always write them letters. I'm going to study to become a computer programmer and then I'd like to go back to China. They need people with skills and I'd like to help.*

## How to Start a Youth Program

1. Get people who believe in God to help. You need about ten to start with.

2. Be patient. You have to spend time to get it going.

3. You need money, so think of a way to get donations.

4. Start with simple, enjoyable activities. From there you can gradually give them knowledge of God.

—Jimmy Cheng and Louie Leung

## Vineyard Fellowship's Most Successful Programs:

- Graduation Dinner Party. All the graduates—from both high school and colleges—are honored at a special dinner. All their families and church members are invited.

- Bring a Friend Day. All the members invite their friends for skits, games, fun. Members will give a testimony also.

- Annual Ice Skating Trip. Again, we invite friends. If they've had a good time, they'll come to church with us.

## Why does it work?

This is a parish that unflinchingly looks to real and important needs of the community and sets about meeting them, using the talents and energies of young adult leaders who serve in important church leadership positions.

# Listening Hearts

## EPISCOPAL SCHOOL

**H**oly Innocents' is described as a school whose "academic expectations are rigorous, commitment to the arts is strong and physical education and athletics are emphasized in encouraging each and every student to reach his/her potential and thus take his/her place as an involved and responsible citizen." Holy Innocents' students are expected to succeed and they do. They are expected to "look good" and they do. They are expected to excel, by their parents, by their school, by their churches, and by the diffuse pressures of the society in which they live. Garrison Keillor would describe these young people as "above average," but northern Atlanta where the school is located is no Lake Wobegon and their lives are far from simple. These young people are no innocents.

Holy Innocents' Episcopal School is a private school operated under the auspices of Holy Innocents' Episcopal Church. Its 1,300 students are mostly Christian and Jewish, but there are a few Muslims in the student body, as well as those with no religious affiliation. According to Chaplain Mike Wallens, "We hope that by the time students leave school, their faith is strengthened, and they are aware of God's presence in their lives, whether they be Jewish, Muslim, Christian, Buddhist, or Hindu."

The attractive and well-equipped school is located on a thirty-three acre campus in north Atlanta. It includes four levels from preschool to upper school. Holy Innocents' is unquestionably competitive, yet its staff is caring and compassionate, and committed to providing students with a rich program in Judeo-Christian traditions. Dr. Susan Groesbeck, formerly "New York State Teacher of the Year" is beginning her first year as the school's head. She is energetic and up-beat and so is the tone of the school.

It was the end of the second day of interviewing and the writer was in the middle of her good-byes at the chaplain's door, when one of the peer counselors, a 15-year-old sophomore, poked her head around the corner. "I just wanted to let you know that Daddy's surgery went well." Her father was miles away at Johns Hopkins Hospital in Baltimore receiving cancer treatments. The student's relief was evident. She smiled as Chaplain Mike Wallens gave her a warm, encouraging hug. The writer recalled that this was the same student who had taken the trouble to come to school early that morning to answer questions about being a peer counselor. She had freely engaged in the topic, never hinting for a moment that she had anything at all on her mind that might preoccupy her. Her courage in the face of a very immediate anxiety crystallized for this writer just how, these young people exhibit courage advantaged as they may be.

In the previous two days the peer counselors talked about the issues they and their peers were facing: illness, the death of a parent, alcoholism, drugs, anorexia, suicide, divorce, getting along with stepparents. These along with the more usual concerns, such as: feeling like an outsider, fitting in to the group, forming friendships, breaking up with a boy/girl friend. Peer Counselor Melissa Hudson, explains that as peer counselors,

> We try to make them feel comfortable and relaxed. We have to be able to listen. We ask open-ended questions to get them talking. We can't solve their problems but we try to lead them to finding their own answers.

The Rev. Mike Wallens came to Holy Innocents' Episcopal School in the summer of 1994 with a mandate to: enhance the spiritual life of the school, work to diversify the student body, and enhance the quality of student life, especially in the upper school (high school). He is head chaplain of a staff that includes three others. He established the peer counseling program at Holy Innocents'. Mike is a bear of a man, big in size and in breadth of character. He is warm and there is depth and wisdom in his eyes. He is not old, yet he has the look of a wise, old, Jewish rabbi whose life has been steeped in prayer and Torah. He is well-qualified for his work. "This is my calling. I've always felt I was called to work with children and youth. It's a calling I've been given by God and I try to be faithful to it." Speaking about the process of peer counseling, Mike says, "It's through our actions that we present God's love. It shows faith and thus people sense there's something more than one human being reaching out to another."

Mike Wallens feels that peer counseling is uniquely suited to young people of high school age because,

> It taps into what is naturally present in the lives of teenagers—compassion, caring, wanting to help, and the willingness to develop relationships. It is the Spirit of God within me reaching out and listening to the Spirit of God in another.

## Peer Counseling

At Holy Innocents' there are twenty-six peer counselors in grades ten through twelve. Students apply to become peer counselors through an application process, which includes supplying references and an interview with Chaplain Mike Wallens and other peer counselors. Having been accepted, they spend somewhere between seventy to a hundred hours in training to prepare for their responsibilities. It is a demanding program, which includes participation in two weekend retreats, follow-up meetings one Sunday afternoon a month, and helping conduct retreats for children in the middle and lower schools.

Training sessions include learning how to listen ("active listening"), how to communicate with others effectively, and how to help others work out their problems. They learn how to examine their own feelings and values, and how to deal with issues that may be presented to them: family, drugs, sexuality, death and loss, pregnancy, peer pressure, AIDS, eating disorders, school problems, suicide, alcoholism, and abuse. They are taught to quickly access the problems they are not qualified to handle, most importantly, whether the person poses a threat to him/herself or others, or is suicidal. Right from the beginning, confidentiality is stressed. Peer counselors are trained to never share with another student what they have been told in trust and confidence.

Following the first stage of training, there is a commissioning service for the peer counselors. In it, the school community, parents, and friends pledge their support to the peer counselors, while the counselors pledge that they will endeavor to carry out their roles with compassion and integrity.

The peer counselors, names, telephone numbers, and hours of availability are published and posted around the school. They are backed up by Mike Wallens, the upper school counselor, a pediatrician, a psychologist, and a social worker on call—professionals who volunteer their professional services to the program.

While most peer counseling entails lending a listening heart and ear to a peer who is experiencing the usual run of life's ups and downs, crisis situations sometimes come up, and the counselors are trained to recognize them when they do. Mike cited that last year there were three suicidal students. One of them came to a peer counselor on a weekend when Mike was away. The peer counselor called the psychologist on call, and the parents were contacted. Later, the student came back and said "Thank you. You saved my life."

Virtually all the peer counselors feel that they are gaining far more than they are giving. The following comments typify a few of the ways the peer counselors feel they are benefiting from their responsibilities:

*"Everything has changed about myself and what is important to me. It's made me a better person. The program makes you become more open and it makes you see things from other vantage points. You also learn a lot about the way you present yourself."*
—Effie Swartwood, age 16, junior

*"Peer counseling is a way of learning to handle situations. You learn to step back from situations. Even if it's your best friend you're counseling with, you have to be objective."*
—Kelly Albritton, age 16, junior

*"It's taught me that there are different ways of looking at situations. I feel I've become a better listener, a better friend. I know myself better. I've become more tolerant and accept that each one of us is different."*
—Russell Flynt, age 17, senior

*"Being a peer counselor has helped me to realize how to and how not to talk to a friend, and how to adjust my flow to theirs."*
—Melissa Hudson, age 18, senior

*"It's made me firm in my beliefs. At the same time, I can accept the strong beliefs of others, if they don't agree with me....I am only intolerant of people who are intolerant."*
—Dylan Deal, age 17, senior

*"I thought I'd just learn how to be a peer counselor, but I also got to know a lot about myself."*

—Sarah Moreland, age 15, sophomore

*"We are like a haven to a lot of people."*

—Erica Barbakow, age 16, junior

Most of the peer counselors believe that the skills learned in the program will help them later on. Kristin Wolford, an 18-year-old senior feels that "In business, any business, you have to be able to work with and get along with all kinds and types of people." Spears Mallis, also an 18-year-old senior, feels that, "In any relationship—at work or in your personal life—you have to be able to be in touch with your feelings."

## Peer Counseling Vis-à-vis Talking Things Over With an Adult

Meghan Kimzey, age 17, senior says:

*Since we're peers we can relate better than adults. We're closer. There's a gap with adults, certain things you just wouldn't want to tell an adult.*

## Why the Peer Counseling Program Is Important

*The peer counseling program is important in schools for several reasons. First, adolescence is a difficult time for everyone with the transition from childhood dependence to true self-sufficiency. Second, life in the 1990s includes a myriad of problems unknown to previous generations. These issues range from drug abuse to teen pregnancy to AIDS. Often teenagers cannot handle these problems on their own, and adults can only do so much. The peer counseling program provides the basis for individuals suffering from any number of difficulties to come for honest counseling from someone their own age. There is a limited amount any one person can handle on their own, and in order to foster a healthy school community we must come together in times of trouble to help each other. This loving help is the foundation of the peer counseling program.*

*The peer counseling program is vitally important here at Holy Innocents'. As a school, we serve in many ways as a microcosm of the turbulent outside world. Certain issues abound here, while others are rare. For instance, eating disorders run rampant in our upper school, while pregnancy is rarely encountered. The peer counselors at Holy Innocents' function to listen, counsel, and support all students during difficult times.*

—Jessica L. Lewis, peer counselor

*Peer counseling provides students with an opportunity to share their feelings in a safe environment. It is only through a conversation with a peer that a student feels total confidentiality. This is not implied responsibility. It is actual responsibility. These students are trained and given the opportunity to provide a valuable service to their classmates. I have been singularly impressed with the caliber of counseling the students offer. They know their boundaries and are clear to engage adult help when needed.*

—Dr. Susan R. Groesbeck, head, Holy Innocents' Episcopal School

## Profiles of Peer Counselors

Several peer counselors talk about their lives and concerns.

**Jessica Lewis**, is a 16-year-old junior and a National Merit Scholar. This year Jessica is taking advanced placement (AP) courses in biology, chemistry, and history. Next year she is planning to take AP courses in English, calculus, physics, Spanish, and art. She plays tennis and the piano. She likes art and writing. She writes for the school newspaper paper. She would like to become a doctor.

*As a peer counselor, I specialize in eating disorders, primarily because of my personal experiences. I'm in the fourth stage of anorexia development.*

*We need to address this issue of anorexia because girls are dying inside. It's difficult to help a person with anorexia because there's nothing the person can do about it until they want to change. I know. I'd have "Egg Beaters" for breakfast. I'd pick at what my mom made for dinner, and I'd drink thirty glasses of water a day....300 calories. I was always cold and always tired.*

*I had to want to change. There's no way I could have made it without family and friends. Not everyone happens to have a wonderful brother and friends like mine, but even if they do, its sometimes hard to talk with them. This is why I'm a peer counselor. I'd hate to have others go through this without a friend to talk to...so much pain, and pain is not what these years of your life are supposed to be.*

*I really like the quote by Rose Kingman, "In the end all that really matters is how you trust each other." I'm so much happier now. There's a big difference. I live a full life...and just think, I might not even have been alive.*

*I'm going to be a doctor and I want to help the community. There's so much wrong in the world. I may not know just what to do but I'm going to get off my butt and try something. We're here to teach what's going on and to be a mirror back to the community. When people go through things, I want to be there for them. There's never going to be a perfect solution, but learning how to work on problems shows one really cares.*

### A Diet of Crackers and Water in a Land of Plenty

Anorexia is a reaction, especially on the part of teenage girls, to a world where they feel society's pressures to be perfect: smart, pretty, witty, a perfect size 8, accomplished, charming, confident, happy, going some place. In a world where they feel like robots controlled by forces in their lives they can do nothing about, the only thing they believe they **can control** is what they eat and drink.

**Brian Yancy**, age 17, is vice president of the junior class. He writes for the school newspaper and plays on the tennis team. He lives in Norcross and attends Christ Episcopal Church. Outside of school, he is very involved in scouting. He is lodge chief of the Order of the Arrow in the Atlanta Area Council. Presently he is completing the requirements to become an Eagle Scout, which include doing a substantial community service project. Brian talks about it and other matters.

*Before you can become an Eagle Scout you have to do a service project, so I built a playground for Rainbow Village, a temporary housing facility for families, supported by Christ Church, Norcross's outreach program. It took a year-and-a-half.*

*I had to get all the supplies. I got all the lumber and hardware donated from a building supply company. Volunteers came from Emory University. They did the initial clearing of the ground and got rid*

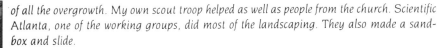

of all the overgrowth. My own scout troop helped as well as people from the church. Scientific Atlanta, one of the working groups, did most of the landscaping. They also made a sandbox and slide.

I was surprised at how the project grew. It showed me that once you get a few people interested in what you believe in, others will want to be involved and contribute.

I think the biggest concern of people my age is the future. A lot of people have the attitude of "I don't know. I don't care." But they're scared. What are they going to be doing and where will they be in ten years? Inside, most of them do care but once they become frustrated they lose hope in what they want to achieve. If I could tell President Clinton one thing about kids my age it would be this: "Kids care about their future but they are sometimes prevented from succeeding because of family and social problems. But the desire is there and you can help them become good citizens."

**Meghan Kimzy**, age 17, is a senior interested in a career in the performing arts. She sings, acts, and dances. Asked why she wanted to become a peer counselor, Meghan laughs..."I've always been a psychologist for my friends!"

People come with boy problems. A friend of mine was having major family problems. Another had a brother who was going to court. Someone else's parents are getting divorced. The mother is putting her under a lot of pressure and she and her mother don't get along anyway. Sometimes a boy wants help in breaking up with his girlfriend. Whatever the problem is, when someone's upset or depressed, I try to get them into better spirits by the time they leave.

Most people just want someone to listen to them and understand where they're coming from, to realize that there's someone on their side.

**Jeremy Stacy**, age 17, is a junior taking advanced placement classes in biology, chemistry, calculus, and English. He is an Episcopalian who attends the Cathedral of St. Philip. He rides and races a mountain bike. Like Brian Yancey, Jeremy is also active in scouting. His Eagle Scout community service project was building an outside classroom for an elementary school in Atlanta.

Through participating in the peer counseling program you find out what is of value to you and just how helpful it is to have a group you can say anything to [other peer counselors]. After my father died, I was in therapy for a while. It made a difference in my life. I really learned the value of therapy and how it can help people.

Anytime someone comes to me, I, as a practice, will pray for them, praying that a solution will be found for their problem. I tell them I'll pray for them.

A friend of mine got atypical pneumonia and a weird infection. He was a cross-country star but he got so bad that now he can't even speak or think. He can only make unintelligible noises. When it started, I told his family I would be praying for him. I know they appreciated it.

There are a lot of atheists in this school. Some students have been raised to interpret the Bible literally, so they look at Bible stories and say "This couldn't possible have happened," and then they reject the whole thing. I try to explain that the Bible isn't meant to be taken literally, but they're so rooted in those beliefs, it's difficult to budge them.

I had a cross from Happening [high school Cursillo]. At a camp I was working at they made me take it off since we weren't supposed to have anything on our uniforms, anything that indicated a religious connection. They told me that they'd give it back but they lost it. This really distressed me.

My faith helps me in counseling people. Anyone of any religion can believe in God's teachings on compassion....My faith gives me a deeper understanding of life.

## A Parent's Perspective...

Elsie Graham says:

My daughter, Jennifer, who graduated last spring was a peer counselor.

What they learn from being peer counselors is life skills. They learn how to listen. They learn how to interpret body language, when and what to say. Peer counseling is the most valuable thing my daughter, Jennifer, learned when she was a student here. If you only knew how many adults have said, "Jenny, can I talk to you about this problem....How would you handle it?"

Today's world is so hard on kids. We have a society of alcohol, violence, family problems. There are so many dysfunctional families. These kids are living in a world of lots of drugs. Parents take drugs. Kids sell them. Just because these kids are in a private school does not mean that they are sheltered from society's problems. They are also pressured. They have to prove themselves and even then, they need a lot of luck to make it.

# Mustard Seeds in God's Garden

## DIOCESAN CAMPUS MINISTRY

T he evening shadows are falling across the prairie grassland. As the hush of the day recedes, the tall grasses are highlighted against the golden setting sun.

Prairie grasses can grow ten feet high and sustain abundant wildlife, including an estimated 400 species of plants, 200 kinds of birds, 29 types of reptiles and amphibians, and 31 species of mammals. The tall grass prairie that greeted westward-moving settlers once covered 140 million acres. Today less than 1 percent of it survives. A piece of it, just west of Manhattan, is set aside as a Quiet Garden and is used as one of the ministry sites of the Episcopal ministry at Kansas State University.

The notion of the Quiet Garden began in England several years ago. A Quiet Garden is a place to be outside for prayer, stillness, and spiritual reflection. An Anglican priest—considering modern people's need to get away to outdoor spaces for rest and refreshment—began asking people who owned such spaces to open them up to the public. The Rev. Cathy Chittenden-Bascom, and her husband, Tim Bascom, campus ministers at Kansas State University (KSU) liked the idea and conceived of it as an outreach ministry of the St. Francis Episcopal Ministry. Tim Bascom's family owns land in Keats, close to the KSU campus and, in addition, their immediate neighbors, Judd and Nancy Swihart, allow people to walk on their land as well. Using both properties, 130 acres are available. In addition to the prairie with its beautiful grasses, the land includes woodlands, gullies, tall trees, and outcroppings of limestone. Cathy Chittenden-Bascom explains,

## Seeing the Environment with the Eyes of God

Meditations for Early Arrivals (2:00-4:00pm)

Find a quiet place by yourself

From where you are, focus on your surrounding environment,

How many different aspects of God's creation can you observe from this one place? Use all you senses - look, listen, smell, and touch.

Write down everything you observe. Don't be concerned about not knowing the names for things.

Find one particular living thing (plant, insect, bird. etc.) that you can closely observe. Write a detailed description of it, noting everything you can observe. Include its relationships with its environment. Be as detailed as possible.

Meditate on the scriptural truth that you are God's appointed steward of that living thing you have just described. How has your observation affected how you think about your stewardship responsibility toward that small piece of God's creation?

**Read Psalm 148**

Take some time to pray, thanking and praising God for the creation surrounding you.

The Quiet Garden is less about flower beds than about the prairie and woodland environments designed by God for the Kansas Flint Hills. Quiet Gardens now extend around the globe where people open their land to others for days of prayer, rest, and spiritual renewal. The Quiet Garden is based on the simple conviction that modern Christians need more opportunities to be alone and to pray like Jesus.

The Quiet Garden is both a ministry and a mission with and to students. It is open to everyone in the community, but students have taken particular responsibility in clearing and creating walking trails, refurbishing an old hermit cabin, and greeting visitors to the garden. A Kansas State landscape architecture professor supervised a student who designed a garden highlighting native plants and grasses.

If one word describes the character of the garden, it would be creativity—God's creativity in nature and the creative expression of human beings. People have come to the Quiet Garden engaged in artistic endeavors of one kind or other. The hermit cabin tucked away in the woods has been used by people writing songs, novels, and sermons. It has served as an artist's studio. Retreats, quiet days, and conferences have been held at the Quiet Garden. St. Francis Canterbury Quiet Garden Scholarships have been established to encourage one or two students each year to pursue special interests in the environment and/or the arts in light of Christian tradition and their own spiritual growth.

This evening, KSU senior and Quiet Garden Scholar, Julie Sinn, and Kail Katzenmeier, a 1995 graduate, take the visitor on a hike through the garden. Julie is just finishing an afternoon's work of trail grooming, and Kail points out clumps of cedar trees, observing that cedars were brought in by settlers for windbreaks, and have spread like weeds throughout the prairie. As we continue, they point out "Le Shack," a cabin on the edge of the prairie, and a chapel further along the path. Julie explains that, as a Quiet Garden Scholar, she both maintains the trails and works on a special study project. She is writing a series of essays on her experience of growing up on a farm, its influences on her life, and what it means to be a modern woman in this time and place. She is exploring, "what the Bible and Christianity are saying to me and how I apply my faith to my daily life."

Even though mustard plants are not native to the Kansas prairie, it is no wonder that Cathy Chittenden-Bascom likes the image of the mustard seed. Here in God's garden, seeds of love, responsibility, joy, and creativity are growing wondrously.

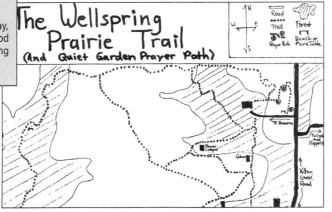

The Wellspring Prairie Trail (And Quiet Garden Prayer Path)

### Canterbury Tales

It is dark now, and as dinner finishes at the Bascom house, students are starting to drift up to "Le Shack" for an evening of Canterbury Tales. They laugh as they stumble along the trail, sharing the one flashlight lighting the path.

Once assembled in the candlelit cabin, with the scent of brewing coffee wafting through the air, Toby Becker, the coordinator of Canterbury Tales, begins.

He reminds the group that tonight is an evening of sharing any sort of creativity, either of their own or others. Toby is an art student and he begins by rolling out the first panel of a triptych he has drawn.

Chad Senuta offers a song he composed. After playing his guitar and singing, he explains that "this is a prayer song based on Psalm 27. I was just thumbing through the psalms and praying that God would help me find something I liked. `If God is for us—who can be against us?'—that was the idea I was looking for." He admits that he is sometimes fearful, but through this psalm and the song he composed based on it, "I could feel God encouraging me."

Julie Sinn reads a story she wrote about herself and Speedy, her childhood friend. Julie Norbury read, "Will You Buy My Package, Please?" a poem she wrote after returning to KSU from a semester in France. It is funny and a bit cynical. Toby comes in again; this time he reads a children's story, *Grandfather's Journey*. He observes that it is not really a kid's story because, like Grandfather, we can never return home again.

Josh Thompson says he is feeling a bit nervous because this is the first time he has shared a Canterbury Tale. He sings a song, accompanying himself on the guitar. It is a song that gives him comfort, especially when he thinks back on his years from twelve to sixteen when he had childhood cancer. The song comforts him when he thinks of the young people he knew who died when they were going through it. He lingers a long time on one phrase, "I'll see you again when the stars fall from the sky."

Lisa Senuta shares what it felt like to be so small overlooking the immensity of the Grand Canyon. "I felt so insignificant. It's strange to be drawn to such a vulnerable feeling...but I was drawn to that sense of vulnerability, which made me feel that everything is a gift from God."

The candle passes to Kail, who sang a song he had composed about his grandfather, "Grandfather Was A Boy Once," in which he tried to remember what the old man, now dead, was like as a child. Quietly he sang, his words penetrating the night and reaching into the hearts of the listeners; listeners silently recalling their own grandpas—"Grandfather, I want you to live on."

Others made their offerings. People quietly came and went. The flashlight finally died, making the small room in the woods even dimmer. Tim Bascom closed off the evening by reading from his quotation book, an idea he has borrowed from his grandmother. A quote from her book became his first entry, "My thought is that to live in the hearts of others is not to die" (Lillian Bascom). Tim observed that what one records in a quotation book says a lot about the keeper of the book. He shared a quote from Vincent Van Gogh, "Christ was more of an artist than others...he worked in living flesh." Then he concluded with the thought that "the winds of God are always blowing, but you have to hoist your sails."

## Why Do It?

*"It's such a creative atmosphere with other Christians. We're all students and I enjoy coming out and sharing the creativity I've had. In another situation someone would say, 'Yes, that's interesting,' and suggest 'Now let's go on to the next item on the agenda.' But here we really listen to each other."*

—Julie Sinn

*"It's a time to share deeply the experiences of what life is."*

—Julie Norbury

*"Humans are very oral, talking with each other, telling stories... This is what makes us human beings; it always has throughout the ages. But it isn't done any more. Here we do it!"*

—Toby Becker

*"I'm a mechanical engineer. If you're an engineer, you've been trained to be a technological nerd. I like to be here to get away from the technological aspects of life. It doesn't matter what's the subject of the meeting, it's the people, and Cathy and Tim especially. They really do care. It's special to me that these people care so much."*

—Josh Thompson

*"It takes some of the science out of life and a night up here in the dark makes me realize that there's more to life than science."*

—Kail Katzenmeier

## The Ministries of St. Francis Canterbury Episcopal Church

- **Quiet Garden**. A quiet place to spend time outdoors, to hike, to pray, and just "be." Also special conferences, retreats, and worship.

- **Canterbury Tales and Coffee**. Twice a month students of St. Francis and friends gather for coffee and the sharing of creativity—songs, poems, drama, paintings, sculpture. Sometimes people share how they do art, or how God and their beliefs influence what they create.

- **Worship**. The heart of all the St. Francis ministries is Sunday evening worship at the Danforth Chapel on the KSU campus. This is the central Christian act, the ancient wisdom of the sacraments, particularly the Holy Eucharist, with music and preaching. Rock and roll rhythms are combined with liturgical chant. The preaching is meant to let the Holy Spirit address each person here and now.

- **Bible Study.**

- **Small Prayer Groups.**

- **Parties**. Parties of all kinds are sponsored by the community. A recent party had the P theme—"People Porting P"—possessions, poodle skirts, popcorn, pretzels, purple pantsuits....

- **Trips**. Trips are for pleasure and to nurture the community. A fall canoe trip is popular.

# The Tales of Canterbury Pilgrims

**Becky Katzenmeier**, age 23, a 1996 graduate of KSU, now a teacher at Junction City High School. "I grew up an Episcopalian and worked to get Episcopal ministry back at KSU in 1992." Becky served on the search committee that recommended Cathy Chittenden-Bascom as campus minister at KSU. "Cathy is a very alive person. Her belief in Jesus and the Holy Spirit are very evident. She is willing to be open to all people and all ideas." Becky goes on to reflect upon what is best about the ministry:

*For me, even though it's an Episcopal service, it is very nondenominational. We have a wide range of traditions, thoughts, and ideas. The strands all come together in a wonderful way through our worship.*

*In the future I'd like a little house, some land, children, and animals. I'd like to stay in Manhattan and always be involved in St. Francis of Canterbury. It's one of the most alive groups I've ever been a part of.*

**Joshua Thompson**, age 23, is a graduate of KSU, with a major in mechanical engineering. Josh is fixing up an old GMC truck and he enjoys "storm chasing," a uniquely prairie pastime.

To look at Josh now, one would never suspect that he is lucky to be alive. He once had a tumor that left him with one-eighth of his lung capacity, and that was doubling in size every 24-48 hours. He talked about his long period of chemotherapy and how every week his blood count test determined whether or not he would be able to go to school on Monday. As a result he lives week to week. "Some people live day by day. I live week by week." Josh tells his story:

*What kept me going was that my family laughed a lot. My brothers, Bill and Ted, kept me going, as well as lots of really good friends. I wasn't the kid with cancer. I was just Josh. Sometimes when tragedy strikes, families split apart. We got closer together.*

*What's hardest of all is talking about my faith in God. All I can say is that God gave me the calmness that made me believe that in the end, everything would be O.K. I never doubted it. I prayed a lot and I started to read the Bible. I read it constantly. I didn't ask why this happened to me, but rather why these things happen at all. I asked myself what I was supposed to learn, what bigger picture do I have to learn from. Not me, but why not me?*

*I try to be a well-rounded person. Technology is fun, that's why I'm an engineer. I like to be outside and in nature. I want to live life to its fullest and find a balance; not too much of this, too little of that. I'd like to have a loving wife and a good family. I want to live in peace and still have fun.*

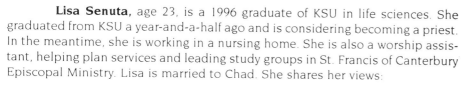

**Lisa Senuta**, age 23, is a 1996 graduate of KSU in life sciences. She graduated from KSU a year-and-a-half ago and is considering becoming a priest. In the meantime, she is working in a nursing home. She is also a worship assistant, helping plan services and leading study groups in St. Francis of Canterbury Episcopal Ministry. Lisa is married to Chad. She shares her views:

*Worship is alive in the Holy Spirit. Our services show people that church can be exciting. We are very diverse and our diversity brings energy. People are challenged, yet we pray together, and our unity in God we express as a group.*

*We want people to feel comfortable with who they are and we're not forcing anyone into any particular Christian mold. Sure, problems come up. There are differences of opinion, of theology, and life experiences that clash, but on the whole it's pretty healthy.*

When asked about heroes and role models, Lisa responded:

*Heroes? Heroes died out during my generation. Being born in the midst of Watergate, my generation says nobody's perfect, everyone's flawed.*

Nonetheless, she has hopes and dreams:

*I hope I will be continually changing, growing, and being challenged to be like Christ. I hope someday my husband and I will be in ordained ministry together. I hope my ministry will be one in which I'm real to people, a sign pointing to something fuller, pointing to God.*

**Paul Gleue**, age 43, a graduate of KSU, is now a graduate student in anthropology. Paul works as a carpenter. "It's just a job," he says.

It is a Saturday morning and today is Paul's birthday. As we meet at the Express Royale, a coffee shop, there is a sense of anticipation in the air. KSU's "Wildcats" are playing their neighbor—the University of Nebraska's football team. KSU has not beaten them in thirty years. The town is full of KSU fans, hoping that this year will be different. The celebration would give Paul a birthday to remember.

Paul is a new member of the Canterbury Episcopal Fellowship. He got involved through playing soccer with Tim Bascom. Shortly after they met, Paul broke his leg. "I couldn't work. I couldn't dance. I couldn't go to my Aikido class. Nothing! Because everything I did involved mobility." Tim reached out to him. Paul says:

*I'm not used to opening up and telling other people about my personal things, but I followed an impulse and just started talking with Tim. He mentioned different things about the church—the Quiet Garden, the Bible discussion group, Canterbury Tales. He made me realize that this church is different.*

*Looking for a church is like buying a car. You have to check out different models, until you get one that suits you.*

Previously, Paul had been a conscientious church member, but...

*I got to the point where I thought I'd learned everything. So what's next? Deeper understandings weren't there. This wasn't a pleasant feeling. In fact it was discouraging because I still hadn't found myself. Where was the me in all that the church teaches? I felt like an outsider just occupying a chair...but I knew somewhere there had to be more.*

*I'm still looking to see where I fit in, but I'm real pleased by what I see in the Canterbury Fellowship. There's something for me.*

He continues:

*I've always been an outsider—from kindergarten on up. I didn't want it that way but I just never discovered the environment I needed. It just wasn't there for me and I never fit in. This has always bothered me but I built up my defenses and said to myself "I don't want to be there. I don't want to participate." Thus I developed ways of keeping people at a distance.*

*So I've been trying to discover ways of being around people. The Bible discussion group puts me in an environment where I have to open up and tell people what I think. Canterbury Tales is another way that helps people be more creative about their thoughts and feelings. It approaches opening up in a different way. They are both ways of telling people who you are.*

Now that the log jam is broken, Paul is looking for ways to: "Talk, talk, talk. I'd rather talk than eat! I don't want to just think it. I'm looking for ways to feel it."

He thinks about what has happened during these last few months and cites the Bible discussion group as being formative along with Tim Bascom's leadership. He says of Tim: "He heals. He creates the atmosphere for people to give expression to their thoughts and feelings, where before they didn't have an opportunity. But it's not just `I feel, I feel that.' Tim pulls it together and gets it relevant. He has a way of healing people. He's an artist!"

## Campus Ministry in the Diocese of Kansas

The foundations for this generation's campus ministry at Kansas State University and the University of Kansas were laid by the Diocese of Kansas and, in particular, the College Work Committee. In 1990-92 both KU and KSU were without chaplains. This period was used as an occasion to re-evaluate and renew a vision for campus ministry. The College Work Committee researched successful ministries on other campuses and wrote the following mission statement:

*The mission of the College Work Committee in the Diocese of Kansas is to provide a Christian presence in the Episcopal-Anglican tradition on the campus of every public institution of higher learning in the diocese, in order to provide pastoral care for students, faculty, administrators, and staff; to provide channels for communication and cooperation between the churches and of the college community itself; to address the needs of society and equip persons to meet those needs.*

They established goals that included establishing full time chaplains at both KU and KSU. These chaplains would be referred to as "Lead Chaplains" and would also work to encourage the development of Episcopal ministries on the other campuses of the state.

Excited about this new beginning, members of the College Work Committee arrived at the 1991 Diocesan Convention wearing buttons bearing the Episcopal Church shield and the words "On Every Campus." They were shocked when the convention voted down their proposals and budget. But a dramatic reversal followed. Becky Katzenmeier explains:

Traude Norman, an 18-year-old KSU student got up and addressed the convention. She told them that "We're a part of the church too. There are students who have no voice and no vote in this convention. I do have a voice and a vote and I want to speak for all the students. We want active ministry at KSU and KU."

Campus ministry was saved that day. With the vote reversed, the initiatives started by the College Work Committee could continue. The Rev. Joe Alford was appointed Episcopal chaplain at the University of Kansas and, in the fall of 1993, the Rev. Cathy Chittenden-Bascom, the Episcopal campus minister at Kansas State University.

The College Work Committee still seeks to extend Episcopal ministry to all universities and colleges throughout the state. The "Lead Chaplain" idea has been greatly modified due to the inviability of travel and real oversight. Instead, professors and other staff in the particular academic communities are being sought to serve as lay ministers organizing ministries relevant to their sites. They serve on and are accountable to the College Work Committee. Even though the original dream of ministry on state campuses has not been fully realized, much has been accomplished, especially at KU and KSU. Dr. Lyn Baker-Norris, KSU professor and former co-chair of the College Work Committee said, "I wanted students' needs to be met. I wanted to make possible an openness to the kind of questioning people have at that time in their lives."

### The Campus Ministers

Lyn Baker-Norris talks about the development of ministry at Kansas State University:

We perceive in Cathy Chittenden-Bascom a level of caring about other people and an ability to engage a spiritual presence. It has remained a wonderful fit. And Tim [Cathy's husband] was a bonus that just came along. We had no expectations that he would be involved.

By profession Tim is a writer. He is also a sculptor. He is a lay person. With the birth of Cathy and Tim's second child, Tim and Cathy are now sharing the role of campus minister—two-thirds time for Cathy and one-third for Tim.

As of 1995 the ministries of both KU and KSU are considered parish ministries, so their chaplains are now rectors.

## What Does It Take to Grow a Solid Campus Ministry?

1. A mustard seed theology. How small a mustard seed is, yet how big the tree it becomes and how beautiful its fruit.

2. Not getting discouraged.

3. Prayer, lots of prayer.

4. Practical support: financial support from the diocese and also the encouragement of the diocesan College Work Committee whose members also serve as advocates and cheerleaders.

5. The willingness to make it a student ministry; letting it germinate in the indigenous culture where students' gifts are valued.

6. The family aspect. We've made the students our friends.

7. Music has been important. Chad, Kail, Christi, Julie and Adam all play the guitar. Sometimes Alex plays the dulcimer. Chad and Kail sometimes compose songs, sometimes they use already published music. We display the music on overheads [overhead projectors]. It is an Episcopal but a hybrid liturgy as far as the music is concerned. They like it.

8. Perseverance.

*—the Rev. Cathy Chittenden-Bascom*

## Mustard Seeds and Butterflies...

Cathy Chittenden-Bascom adds:

The Quiet Garden provides an image of ministry. It's very hard to grow anything out there on the prairie, but for me this fits all kinds of images. Prairie plants have been an inspiration to me about campus ministry. When you plant anything you need to have perseverance. Growing takes time. It takes care and nurture. Ministry has to have deep roots in order to flourish. It might take years for them to grow. The garden suggests servanthood. Maybe we even serve the Creator and creatures in the garden. Last summer the butterflies were wonderful....

# Building Bridges in the Heartland

## DIOCESAN ECUMENICAL CAMPUS MINISTRY

**D**orothy was looking for the yellow brick road that would lead her back home to Kansas. She would not have found it in Lawrence; instead she would have discovered bridges: the bridge between the student community and the poor, the bridge joining Lutheran and Episcopal traditions, and the bridge to the heart, binding together students living in an intentional residential community patterned on a modified Benedictine Rule. There are other ministries of the Episcopal/Lutheran Campus Center at the University of Kansas, but these three form the basic core. The center where the bridges converge is the Episcopal/Lutheran Center, called Canterbury House, consisting of a large house purchased for $1 in 1959 and a chapel—St. Anslem's—that was once the parish hall of a church in Tonganoxie.

### Episcopal/Lutheran Campus Center—The Bridge to Community

While Lutheran and Episcopal bishops were meeting in the mountains of Pennsylvania talking about drawing closer together and eventual full communion, Lutheran and Episcopal students at KU were already living a shared community of faith.

Unlike the Lutherans, the Episcopalians have a house, Canterbury House, and a chapel close to the campus. The Lutheran campus minister, the Rev. Brian Johnson, was dissatisfied with the facilities available to him as a denominational chaplain located in an ecumenical campus ministry office. While he was searching for alternatives, he struck up a friendship with the Rev. Joe Alford, the Episcopal chaplain at the university, and together they negotiated a space-sharing arrangement at Canterbury House.

The two chaplains were well-matched in terms of disposition—easy going, friendly, and perhaps most importantly, they both had a sense of humor. Both shared a concern for the spiritual growth of their students and a keen appreciation for liturgy.

Johnson began renting space at Canterbury House and the two shared the cost of an administrator. These were the first steps. Soon afterward, the two faith communities began sharing worship space in the adjoining St. Anslem's Chapel on Sunday evenings. The Episcopalians had their liturgy at 5:00, followed by a shared meal with the Lutherans at 6:00. Afterward, the Lutherans had their service at 7:00. But friendships grew, not only between the two chaplains but among the students who wanted to share more. Thus, with their chaplains, they began a joint community dinner on Tuesday evenings and later instituted a service in the Taizé pattern. Its ecumenical character made it an inspired choice for the Lawrence community. Taizé is an ecumenical community in France drawing together people of many traditions in a distinctive style of worship characterized by silence, meditation, and the singing of simple songs in a variety of languages, songs that are repetitive and conducive to meditation.

TAIZÉ

Give glory to God, all the earth

Sharing programs and services has helped the students become more appreciative of their own traditions while growing in understanding of the other. "Sharing together," Chaplain Johnson noted, "crystallizes for students who they are as members of a denomination, but it also helps them to be more tolerant." Chaplain Alford adds that, "Each program we share together invests people more and helps them understand themselves and each other better." According to Jon Lassman, a Lutheran student, "For me, the importance is that we're working together and all the differences between the denominations now seem trivial."

The Episcopal/Lutheran relationship has grown quickly from friendship to courtship to marriage. First talks of collaboration began in April, 1994. In Lent, 1996 Lutheran and Episcopal students shared a joint study group and in the Holy Week that followed shared everything together, including a particularly wonderful Good Friday Stations of the Cross. Artists (representing the theater, visual arts, etc.) from around the university were invited to interpret the various stations. For the thirteenth station—Jesus is taken down from the cross—everyone was asked to go outside. They stood quietly as two 75-pound sandbags—what Jesus would have weighed—were carefully lowered from the roof of the building. This service profoundly affected all who attended and it was followed by a joyous Easter celebration. As of the beginning of the 1996 academic year, all programs, services, and projects are entered into jointly.

The shared Lutheran/Episcopal community began with the friendship between an Episcopal priest, the Rev. Joe Alford, and the Evangelical Lutheran Church pastor, the Rev. Brian Johnson. But what would happen if one of them should leave? Anticipating such an eventuality, a clause was added to the joint Letter of Agreement, which authorizes the remaining chaplain to serve on the search committee of the other tradition in seeking a new chaplain. This has proved essential because Brian Johnson has left KU for another calling. Father Alford is serving in the search process for his replacement. In the meantime, Genelle Genkinger is serving as Lutheran interim lay associate, working with Joe Alford, to strengthen the ties as Lutherans and Episcopalians continue to build bridges and pass over them, discovering and appreciating along the way, the riches of each other's tradition.

## From the Mountain Laurel Communiqué

Many years of thorough and conscientious dialogue have brought us to this moment....As we move forward together...We believe that we are being summoned anew to embrace more completely our unity in faith. We believe that our churches are being called to journey in the one apostolic faith together. We rejoice that we have been reconciled to God, and we pledge ourselves to our reconciliation with one another in the mission God now sets before us on this threshold of a new millennium.

—H. George Anderson, presiding bishop of the Evangelical Lutheran Church in America
—Edmond L. Browning, presiding bishop of the Episcopal Church in the USA

## The Jubilee Café—the Bridge to the Street

The Jubilee Café is just like any other restaurant, except that it opens only one day a week for breakfast; and its patrons, who are either homeless or living on very modest means, eat free.

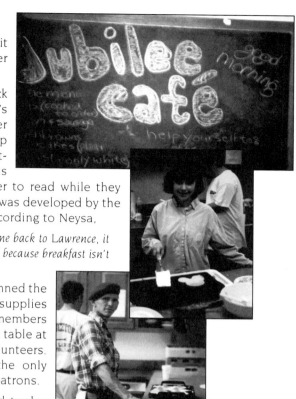

The idea of the café came when KU student Neysa Koury was back home in Iowa City, a university community similar to Lawrence. Neysa's mother was a volunteer at the Agapé Café and Neysa decided to help her out. The concept was a new one to her in that it was not a traditional soup kitchen where guests were all served the same meal—donated food, leftovers and such—this was a café where patrons ordered from a menu items that were freshly cooked for them. They selected a morning newspaper to read while they sipped their coffee. Coincidentally, the breakfast café model in Iowa City was developed by the Rev. Julia Easley who had been an interim chaplain at KU in 1991-92. According to Neysa,

> I thought it was a more dignified approach to serve people in need. After I came back to Lawrence, it just seemed like something that would really go over well here, and it's needed because breakfast isn't usually offered for the people.

Neysa approached Joe Alford with the idea and together they planned the next steps. They would need a central location for the café, money for supplies and volunteers. Joe sold the idea to Trinity Episcopal Church, whose members readily agreed to the use of their kitchen and hall. Neysa and Joe set up a table at the Student Union during Volunteer Week and they advertised for volunteers. Seventy-five students signed up. Aside from taking basic training, the only requirement was that they be willing to sit down and socialize with the patrons.

The café opened its doors on October 18, 1994 when it served twelve meals for its Grand Opening. Now upwards of sixty meals are served every week by a cadre of loyal volunteers who don't mind too much setting the alarm clock early on café mornings.

"I wanted a place that students could run themselves and be in charge," observed Joe. "I didn't—forgive me—want a bunch of retired professors but an entirely student-run organization. This has worked." But Joe had wanted theological reflection groups during which the students could discuss the theological significance of what they are doing. It did not work. According to Joe, "You don't do it unless students want to do it. That's a cardinal rule." Now, two years later, the students do want it. They do not call the meetings "theological reflection groups," but they have set up meetings to talk about their experiences and what they are learning by serving patrons of the Jubilee Café.

## Faces in the Café Crowd

**Neysa Koury**, a 1996 graduate of KU in social work, now a social worker in Kansas City, says:

> I met Joe and he immediately impressed me. [From an Orthodox background] I didn't want to get in with a bunch of 'Bible bangers.' I had a negative stereotype of priests, but Joe was completely accepting and I knew from the start that it would be easy to work with him.

Neysa noted that lots of volunteers are social work majors, yet they have learned quite a bit at the café that is never taught in school. The café gives them a clearer look at the less fortunate and the various social influences that affect people. "For a start," she says, "our clients walk every place. They carry everything they own with them in bags."

Neysa has become friendly with many who live on the streets and she talks about one of her friends, Leon:

> I trusted Leon by instinct. He's a middle-aged man, well-known around Lawrence. He helps many people. He baby-sits. He's raised more kids! As we'd walk around he'd proudly point out "my kids," most of them now grown up. "O Neysa," he'd say, "This is one of my babies." He hung out at my house. When I went away he'd come in and feed my cat.

**Clark Keffer**, is a graduate student in the School of Religious Studies. Clark is a bridge between the café volunteers and the community. A native of Lawrence, his local knowledge has been very useful at times. Fifteen years ago he lost the use of his left arm in a motorcycle accident. He lives on a monthly disability check and does many things. He is an artist and a sculptor and he rebuilds Volkswagens in his spare time.

> I did my oracle that morning and it said I should put myself out more. I was thinking about this and then I was walking through the Union and I saw the Jubilee Café sign-up table. So I signed up. Just like that. Here was this new thing that was starting. I liked the way of providing service. I'd eaten at soup kitchens and I'd been put off. I've been on the receiving end so, trust me, I know the difference between this and a soup kitchen where they're dealing with such a volume of people it becomes mechanized.

> I am from Lawrence and I know many of the people who come to the café. They know me too and we respect each other.

> Not everyone who comes here is homeless. Lots of people work but it's seasonal work. There's one family that comes, mother and father and two sons. They collect cans and sell scrap.

> I quit drinking fourteen years ago. I used to live in darkness but now I live in the light of amazing grace. I am trying to give my life to the Lord and that takes me all sorts of places. I try to use my experience to help those around me. I always try to be part of the answer and go towards the light. I used to be a musician before the accident and when I stopped I had lots of problems. But now I paint. I can get lost in a picture like I used to get lost in music. People tell me I should get serious with it, but I tell them I'm into making art, not selling it.

> I don't think about money. Maybe I'm not American enough! I get by on Social Security. Some of our clients at the café make more than I do. Poverty's an attitude. I have a full, very cool, happy, rich life on less than $1,000 a month total. It's God's saving grace.

**Susie Wilcox**, age 20, is a senior, a life-long Episcopalian from Chicago. Susie was one of the café's first volunteers and does it because, "I'm just called to community service." She explains that she had begun to feel that "God didn't have any part in my life. I'd lost my personal relationship with a higher being. I just couldn't feel it any more." But two experiences are helping her to "begin to feel it again," working in the Diocese of Chicago's summer camp with a wide diversity of children, and volunteering at the Jubilee Café.

> I'd always prayed that I'd feel it and then it just happened. I began to feel it. When I'm with the campers or the guests of the café I'm beginning to see God in them. I am amazed at all the forces in society that are working against them, yet they are so happy and so determined to keep on going and find work.

> Really, it's true. Before the café and the camp, I never knew anything about black culture. Now I'm learning. Now I'm beginning to feel God again.

## The Benedictine Community—Bridge to the Heart

For a long time students have been living at Canterbury House, but now for the first time it is an intentional community of students who live together around the focal points of prayer, work, and study. Four students (Episcopalian, Lutheran, and Roman Catholic) are living in the house, and there are associates who live elsewhere but still participate in the three-fold ideals of the Rule of St. Benedict—work, study, and prayer. They take turns leading daily worship, they work ten hours a week at the Jubilee Café and elsewhere in the community, and they participate in the upkeep of Canterbury House. They study together and share meals.

Last year Canterbury House received a United Thank Offering grant to refurbish and remodel the house, making it a more comfortable home for the community. Dan Bednarczyk, one of the community members who has done a lot of construction work, rewired the house last summer. Other members have been using their skills to remodel it. Jolinda Matthew's father came one weekend and left having laid a new lawn.

"Every student is struggling with what God is calling them to do," notes Joe Alford. "Students know their questions will be respected." Amy Luebbers, a Roman Catholic community member, appreciates this approach. "I came here really wanting to live in community. I liked all the people I talked to. It's a very nurturing environment for me since I've been religiously questioning these last few years."

## Profiles of Community Members

**Jon Lassman,** age 24, a Lutheran, is a 1996 graduate of KU, now a student teacher working in a fourth grade class in Kansas City.

> My first three years at KU I wasn't involved with a church group. I was searching for a way to get involved and then I met Brian Johnson [the Lutheran chaplain] who suggested the community as a way for me to get re-involved.
>
> This community gave me lots of friendships. It got me back into the church, and the fact it was ecumenical was good because it broadened my horizons. Now when I go back home to where I grew up it's kind of boring.

**Jolinda Matthews** is just finishing up at KU. She works at the Glass Onion Café and participates as an associate member of the community. She is a delegate to the World Student Christian Federation. One of her most valuable experiences was last year's Alternative Spring Break trip to New York City where KU students spent spring vacation working in a homeless shelter and a soup kitchen.

> When we told people what we were doing they asked, "Why aren't you in Florida on a beach?" They were flabbergasted when we said we wanted to be there.
>
> The trip took us out of our comfortable elements. We noticed differences between how Lutheran and Episcopal students reacted to different facets of the trip. We had to work through differences with how we felt the church should function in society, such as in the South Bronx. Some of the Lutherans questioned whether the church ought to be running soup kitchens. We also visited the traditional, wealthy Episcopal Church, New York City version, in all its splendor. This kind of opulence shocked the Lutherans. That's something else we had to work through.

**Genelle Genkinger**, age 23, Lutheran Interim Lay Associate, is a 1995 graduate of Luther College. She came to KU to do a master's degree in speech pathology. Last year she was an associate in Canterbury House.

*I moved to Kansas not knowing one person in the whole state. I had no family or friends here. At Luther there were 2,500 students total, so Lawrence felt completely overwhelming.*

*It was the day before classes began and I was going to pay my fees at the center when I noticed the Lutheran/Episcopal table set up there. Brian Johnson told me they were setting up a community at Canterbury House and suggested I come by and have a look. Immediately I felt welcome.*

*Second semester I was offered a job organizing undergraduate outreach and it was becoming clear to me that I was being called to the ordained ministry. This was a tremendous struggle because I liked what I was doing. I liked my courses. But I was listening to the call. In fact I was planning to go to seminary this fall but with Pastor Brian leaving, this position was offered to me. I took it. I thought I could use the experience and I'm glad I did because now I feel much more focused and ready to dig into theology next year.*

*Going through the vocational questioning process in this community has been totally affirming. The members helped me see my gifts and explore my faith. Ultimately I want to find a place where I can fit in and use my gifts to help people.*

**Dan Bednarczyk**, is a 1996 graduate of KU with a B.S. in genetics, now applying to dental schools.

*I've always been involved in my church. I was director of "Happening," the diocesan high school youth program. Church is important to me.*

Genelle suggests that maybe Dan also ought to consider the ordained ministry, but he brushes the suggestion aside.

*She's wrong! I'm a good listener, but no, I'm exercising my faith in other ways!*

*I was headed for a master's in genetics, but I decided it wasn't for me. I'm really good with my hands and this is necessary in dentistry. [He's the student who re-wired the house and has done much of the remodeling.] Look at orthodontistry. It's really a work of construction. You devise a plan and follow it through.*

*I enjoy living in the house and I hope my little brother and sister can come live here some day.*

**Marc Yergovich**, age 22, the oldest of five children, is from Benicia, California. He has a double major in Latin American studies and cultural geography, and he works part-time at the Bourgeois Pig Café. A "cradle atheist," he is now an aspirant for holy orders in the Diocese of Northern California.

*I was deeply impressed with two movies I saw, both about Latin America: "The Mission" and "Romero," about the martyred archbishop of San Salvador, Oscar Romero. I went to El Salvador for six weeks to visit Lawrence's sister city, El Papaturo. This is a resettlement community. I went by myself and I had to depend on myself.*

*What I saw in El Salvador was a completely different way of life. The people didn't have anything. Everyone's poor and the experience of seeing it myself gave me a whole different perception of poverty...the smallest things in life become so valuable.*

*I found my faith in El Salvador. While I was there I just found myself praying. I started doing the Daily Office and if I missed one, I felt so alone.*

*This experience was scary and strengthening at the same time. Many times I had to defend my beliefs, and as I did so, they were strengthened. They assume you're a Catholic so I had to think a lot about what it meant to be an Episcopalian.*

Marc is considering the ordained ministry and right now is going through the discernment process. He is asked why he thinks about ordination.

*Why? I ask myself that every day. It's a question that just won't go away.*

## Quotable Quotes from Joe Alford

"I really want students to wrestle with their faith. They have to be so willing to do it that they might risk losing what's been handed to them."

"I don't quite trust people who never considered rejecting the faith."

"I want to create a place where students can feel safe and supported in their search for God, wherever it might lead them."

"The role of this community in the college setting is to promote questions, to challenge the way we used to worship with our families, and to promote spiritual growth to a totally different and deeper place."

## Creative Campus Ministry—What Does it Take to Make it Happen?

Joe Alford believes:

1. You have to listen to the students and you have to go with them wherever their search takes them. You have to be like a midwife who knows when to tell the mother to push and when to hold back.

2. You have to remember you are on their time and not on your own.

3. You have to forget about numbers, or about making a name for yourself. Campus ministry is always on the margins.

# The Episcopal Church Welcomes You

## DIOCESAN CAMPUS MINISTRY

T he Episcopal Church Welcomes You!" It is a warm welcome from the heart in the heart of a stark, brick, windswept campus. It is usually accompanied by a steaming cup of fresh coffee and often by a meal— waffles, pizza, chocolate chip cookies with succulent, melting chips. It is all here in this Episcopal drop-in center nestled amid Pizza Hut, Burger King, a CVS pharmacy, a copy shop, travel agency, insurance company, a car rental agency, a hair dressing and manicure salon, and the university bookstore. The door is always open. Drawn to a ministry by the scent of home cooking? It, and much more, attracts the students.

At first, it is a little surprising. One does a double take because you do not often see the Episcopal Church in such a commercial setting. This is the Commons, situated on the North Campus of SUNY at Buffalo—two square miles of sterile, plain, modern buildings set in a wide-open space amid a sea of parking lots. More commonly referred to as UB (University at Buffalo), the private university bearing that name was added to the SUNY system in 1962. It is the largest and most comprehensive of the SUNY campuses and a very fortuitous location for the Diocese of Western New York to have made a new start in campus ministry.

### A New Start

After years of ups and downs and the ebb and flow — mostly ebb—of funding, the diocesan Commission on Campus Ministry had enough money and vision to begin from scratch. Thus, during the summer of 1994 the Episcopal Campus Ministry opened its doors in the UB Commons. Unlike the rest of the campus, the Commons is built in a horseshoe formation around a central courtyard, and has an inviting look to it. The location could hardly be better, for in this large commuter college of 25,000 students there is almost no place to congregate except in the Student Union and the Commons. They come to the Commons to shop, eat, make copies, visit one of the businesses, and to pass the time between classes.

The Rev. Beverly Moore-Tasy was called as chaplain, to serve primarily at UB, but also part-time at Niagara University and at SUNY College at Fredonia. Beverly has lots of personal charisma and immediately began attracting students, students who were mostly like herself, African American. Early on she met Linda Wilson, also gifted with a warm, outgoing personality, whom she asked to became the administrator of the Episcopal Campus Ministry at UB. Linda is well-connected in the university through being a native of Buffalo and through her husband who was, until recently, one of UB's football coaches. Linda is European American, so by color, contrast, and connections, the two were complementary.

This is a critically important ministry. A recent study reported in the *Journal of Blacks in Higher Education* found that only ten public institutions had graduation rates of more than 50 percent for black students. In all others surveyed, the majority of black students do not graduate within six years. (*The New York Times*, Dec. 1, 1996.)

The students were alerted to the new ministry at orientation, where there was an information table, and Beverly and Linda were available to talk to students about the center. And they started cooking.

A core group quickly developed and continued to grow as core students brought their friends. Very few were Episcopalians and most of them were black. They came primarily because of the warm hospitality, for Bible study, for meals. They came to meet their friends and make new ones. They came for support, for a quiet place to study, for help with their classes, and for counseling. Beverly and Linda also became advocates and mediators. When a student needed help in settling a matter with a professor, Linda would hear the case and, at times, intercede for the student.

Beverly became the informal chaplain to minority students. At Fredonia State, when racial and ethnic slurs began appearing in classrooms, in the library, in crude graffiti slogans spray painted on walls, culminating in the burning of a cross on the campus, she worked with college administrators to mediate the crisis.

The Episcopal welcome was effective. The drop-in center was working. Thus it was a shock when Beverly announced her resignation last summer (because her husband could not find employment in Buffalo). The loss has been ameliorated by Linda, who has continued to coordinate the ministry on her own, to build and develop it. Linda has worked to increase the ministry's visibility in the diocese and in the university. In the university, she is secretary of the Campus Ministry Association, which gives her a leadership role among the coalition of campus ministers. She is a natural at public relations and has gained a place for the Episcopal Campus Center on the University of Buffalo campus.

## My Goals for This Ministry

1. I want to make Episcopal Campus Ministry more visible in the diocese. The more visible we are, the more solid funding for it will become possible. We will do this through continuing to have a campus ministry table at the diocesan convention and through articles in the diocesan newspaper.

2. I want to make campus ministry more visible in the university through more articles in *Spectrum*, the university newspaper, and through my participating on various university committees. I will continue to be a part of freshman orientation activities. We will have a table in the rotunda during exam weeks with cookies and coffee.

3. I want to increase the involvement of the churches bordering the campus. We are neighbors!

4. I want the students to keep it alive and continue to welcome everyone.

—Linda Wilson, administrator, Episcopal Campus Ministry

## Profiles of People Who Make the Ministry

**Shelly DuBose**, age 24, is a junior majoring is interdisciplinary social sciences/legal studies.

*So why am I here? It's a great atmosphere. My best friends at the university I met here. I've been here ever since the center opened. I was the first person to meet Beverly on campus and I introduced her to everyone else. We've been a close group ever since.*

*I have eleven sisters and brothers. My father died when I was twelve. This forced my mother on to public assistance. I admire her more than anyone else in the world. She's second only to God. She's still raising kids—my sister's four kids. She's taught me strength, discipline, self-worth, and to be proud.*

*My goal is to become a lawyer and to work in family law. I want to help my community and especially the kids. I want them to see that I'm just like them. I want to be an example and to let them know we're not all stars, just ordinary people who have worth.*

*I try to treat people like I want to be treated. I try to treat everyone with respect. I was born a Pentecostalist, but philosophically I'm nondenominational. I'm not a religious person. God isn't a religion. I equate God with love, and I try to show as much of it as I can.*

**Julio Martinez**, age 21, is a senior majoring in finance. Julio also works for AmeriCorps (see sidebar) and part-time for the Episcopal Campus Ministry keeping records.

*My good friend introduced me to Beverly. I met her in the foyer of the Commons and I could tell immediately that she was like a mother figure I could talk to about anything. I needed a lot of help and she gave it to me.*

*I was born living on the street. My parents were homeless. They were living in a car. My grandparents didn't help; there was no such thing as an extended family. My father was always working but we*

### AmeriCorps

AmeriCorps is the "domestic Peace Corps" program initiated by President Clinton. AmeriCorps has 25,000 members working in 438 communities. AmeriCorps members mentor inner-city school children, build playgrounds in empty lots, construct low-income houses, serve meals to AIDS patients, assist the elderly, counsel domestic violence victims, and a host of other community-building activities.

The term is two years. Participants receive an annual living allowance of $7,640, health insurance, and up to two education awards of $4,725.

were always having a hard time. We lived like this for a year-and-a-half and then we moved into a studio in the projects.

I went to Albion State on a football and track scholarship but I was injured my freshman year so I couldn't stay. The guy in "Hoop Dreams" was more stable than me!

I work for AmeriCorps in a program called Athletes in Service in Education. This is a mentoring program of athletes who teach multi-cultural diversity. I go to Bennett High School and St. Joseph's Catholic High School and do workshops. I talk to the kids. I teach them why racism is wrong, why we shouldn't do violence and the importance of education.

Success to me is accomplishing my goals and I haven't accomplished them all yet. I just want to get my B.A. in finance and management and then go right on to get my M.B.A. I'm interested in sports administration.

What motivates me? It's simple. Failure. I don't ever want to go back to living in a car. I don't want my children to have to go through what I went through.

Through satisfying other people I satisfy myself. Isn't that what life should be?

**John Plasir**, age 20, is a sophomore from New York City and a political science major.

I'm a newcomer. I'm here because of my roommate and Julio (previous profile). They said it was a nice place to come—to chat, to study. So I came to see what was going on.

I want to be a lawyer and I think I can work within the system. I know the streets. People in the higher systems don't know what's going on. But it's not criminal justice I'm interested in, it's civil rights— women's rights, the rights of minority people. People's rights are violated all the time. I'm the type of person who will cite something you can't do—like you can't infringe on this person's rights.

**Moselle Whitehead**, age 21, is a sophomore majoring in English.

When I was born they just saw a big white face and dimples. I've been nick-named "Dimples" ever since.

Life has taught me a lot. My mother died in 1984. I was living in Cleveland but found out my real father was in Buffalo. He loved music and sent me tapes but I never saw him. Finally I came to live with him and my stepmother. It was shaky for a while. I grew up fast. I had to learn a lot of things on my own. But I grew to appreciate her. She was there for me. My father isn't the perfect "Huxtable father," but he loves me to death. He's got a picture of me in his Cadillac and tells everyone "This is my baby."

I'd like to be successful. I'd like to have a home where I can stand on the porch and see couples walking on the beach. To fall asleep to the sound of the rushing waves on the sand. That's my dream.

My cousin, Chamyne, in Charlotte, is my role model. She went through school, graduated and has an excellent job. She got married to Craig and had a baby. They bought a house. She did everything straight and in sequence. I'm proud of her. When I got out of high school, she gave me the inspiration to go to college. I'm going to graduate myself now and become a teacher to help children.

I've learned that even when things get rough it doesn't mean it's all over. My mother died and I just cried and cried. I wanted to go with her. But when I got older I realized that life goes on and that I can be somebody. If I had to give anyone advice I'd just tell them to have faith and work hard.

**Larry Neely**, age 26, is a senior majoring in photography. Larry owns his own photography studio and has taken some of the pictures for this chapter.

*I'm a member of the Rastafari religion. There's no church for my religion on campus, so I come here. But if you believe God is universal, if you have faith, you can find knowledge in someone else who has faith. I find that to be true right here. One of the goals of Rastafarianism is to uplift people of color, but I don't get philosophical. All I believe is that if anyone has faith and seeks God's pleasures, they'll be united with him in the hereafter.*

**Tanika Edwards**, age 20, is a junior majoring in environmental design.

*I've been here right from the beginning. I met Beverly in the summer at the Educational Opportunity Program (pre-collage orientation, or EOP). She was warm, quiet, with a very inviting personality. She was generous. We'd take trips together—to Cornell, Washington....We had dinners at her house. We did all the family stuff. We'd meet, sit down, talk....*

*My mother is my role model. She's raising three children herself (me, my little sister Asya, who's 15, and my twin brother, Mikal, also a UB student). And besides that she's putting herself through college.*

*My mother has a firm belief in God and she believes that being successful in life doesn't necessarily mean making a lot of money. She's taught me that if people use their gifts and talents, they'll be successful in whatever they do.*

*I've always wanted to do community work and to contribute to the changing of our world. God is the focus of my life. If God is at the head of it most things are going to fall into place. When you focus on someone as great as God, there's nothing you can't do.*

**Teraysa Smith**, age 19, is a junior majoring in health and human services. Teraysa was prepared for baptism by the Rev. Beverly Moore-Tasy, who is her godmother. She is a member of the Episcopal Student Leadership Team, which planned the 1996 National Student Gathering. Teraysa sings in the University of Buffalo Gospel Choir. She has a four-year-old daughter.

*When I first came here I was searching. I was looking for myself. I met Beverly and she took me and made me understand who Teraysa was. She was like a mother. She helped me realize that I can accomplish something.*

*I want to make a better life for me and my daughter, Deja. She's an angel! It's not about me any more. It's about me and her. I have someone else to take care of and I want to do it right.*

## Quotable Quotes

"If youth were more excited about God, there wouldn't be a Generation X."
—Tanika Edwards, UB junior

"Faith at Work—it's how you carry yourself, the interest you show in others. It's fairness, understanding, compassion to individuals, groups, situations. You have to be what you say you are. Through it your faith is transmitted to others."
—Dennis Black, dean of students

## Support for Campus Ministry

### In the Diocese

The bishop, the Rt. Rev. David Bowman, has been very supportive of campus ministry right from the beginning of his Episcopal ministry and personally raised funds for its support. In 1988, when the United Thank Offering celebrated its one-hundredth birthday at the Detroit General Convention by giving gifts to each diocese of $1,500 to begin new mission ventures, Bishop Bowman designated UTO's gift to the Diocese of Western New York for campus ministry.

The diocese expresses its support for the ministry through the work of its Commission on Campus Ministry. Members include clergy and laity, some from parishes adjoining campuses, along with others who have experience in the academic community. For example, the Rev. David Selzer was the Episcopal chaplain at the University of Minnesota for twelve years before coming to the Diocese of Western New York.

### In the University

There are a number of well-placed Episcopalians among UB's faculty and staff, who are convinced of the value of the Episcopal Campus Ministry in the university venue. These include Dennis Black, dean of students, and Rita Hamilton, an administrator.

### Concern

Campus ministry is not a regular line item in the diocesan budget, and so maintaining an adequate level of funding is a continuing concern.

## The Episcopal Church Welcomes You

The Tin Man—the rather cold, sterile North Campus of the University at Buffalo—has a warm heart, and it is called the Episcopal Campus Ministry. It is a Table of Life and its guests are feasting at a banquet.

# No Longer Strangers

## CONGREGATIONAL OUTREACH

Tonight the menu is a combination of Malaysian, Italian, and American specialties—crostini, an Italian hors-d'oeuvre; and chicken kurma, a Malaysian dish served over basmati rice and salad. The dessert is 100 percent American brownies. The cook is Syed Albukhary, a Muslim, whose family is building a museum of Muslim culture in Kuala Lumpur. Syed is in Florence taking courses in museum administration and will manage the museum when he returns home. Serving others is as much a part of Muslim tradition as it is Christian, thus Syed is here cooking dinner for visiting students at an American Episcopal church.

Every Wednesday night during the academic year the student community of Florence is invited to St. James Church for a program on an aspect of Italian life not likely to be covered in the study abroad programs, or issues related to being a student far away from home. Following the program, the students tuck into a delicious, home-cooked meal at an affordable price.

The sixty to eighty students who show up on a Wednesday night at St. James Church are some of the 5,000 to 7,000 young people who come to Florence for anything from one month to a year. Most typical is a semester abroad, three or four months. There are 35-40 college programs in Florence. Georgetown and Stanford have their own villas where students live and study, but the others live in apartments, with Italian host families, and in student hotels.

Florence is to art history majors what an elegant toy store is to an eight-year-old. The museums, the churches and chapels, the villas and grand plazas, the graceful bridges over the Arno—all this, in addition to the narrow, cobbled streets, pastel-colored buildings, terra cotta tiled roofs, wrought iron lanterns, make Florence one of the most important cities of the European art world, if not the most important. Students come to study Florence's artistic treasures, to learn Italian, and to immerse themselves in the life of another country.

Wonderful as this all may be, it isn't easy to plunge oneself into another culture. For many, it is a first experience of living in a foreign land. It can be a struggle speaking Italian with a host family every evening over dinner. It is hard to find words to ask the most simple things. Just plain talking, which is taken for granted at home, does not come naturally when one is trying to say it all in Italian. It can be frustrating. The worst thing about living in Italy, according to Karen Wardzala, "...is when you need something fixed, and you don't speak the language, and you wouldn't know what to tell them when you did get hold of them....When you finally reach the plumber and he says he'll be right over and doesn't come for two days....When there's no such thing as an appointment anyway and he'll come and go as he pleases....And it's winter and you can't flush the toilet and the heat doesn't work."

Some of the student-abroad programs are small, and it can be difficult to meet a range of English-speaking students. Lots of students just want a home-cooked meal and to feel welcome in a

relaxed environment, the way Mom, either real or imagined, would treat them. "These Wednesday nights," reflected Cate Mellen, "really make a fundamental difference to us. Once a week we have a tie with the USA. Maybe we have a plumbing problem, maybe we just want to speak English, maybe we want to meet a friend, whatever it is, these dinners are a link back to the States....And tonight look what we're having for dessert—brownies!"

Tonight's program also includes the making and judging of Halloween masks. A few of the students have come in full costume. Lots of laughs are shared as students create Madonna, Pippy Long Stocking, Pac Man, and Bart Simpson. Judges Peter Casparian and John Spike confer and decide that everyone deserves a prize: Syed's Malaysian meal, which is now being set out on the serving tables.

"The seder is the underlying theology of International Youth dinners," explains the Rev. Peter Casparian, St. James' rector. "Why do we celebrate tonight?," asks Casparian. "Because we are all strangers and foreigners in a strange land. The seder becomes the Lord's Supper, becomes International Youth on a Wednesday evening."

Casparian continues, What this congregation is about is the ministry to the traveler, a ministry to those who are making a home in a distant place. Almost everyone in the congregation at one time came from a different place. They come to Florence to study, as academics on sabbatical, and students on study abroad programs. They come as refugees, expelled from their countries of origin. Whatever their situation, Jesus is always appearing at the gate—sometimes he appears as a street person, a jobless Albanian [the church also gives away clothes and has a feeding program for the homeless], and sometimes he appears as a preppy American, art history student.

## Leaves from the Cookbook of Wednesday Night Programs

- Italian Culture and Society
- Stereotypes, Norms, and Attitudes
- Florentine Families
- A Taste of Italy
- The Archaeology of Florence
- A Traveler's Italy
- Culture Shock
- Italy and Italians in English Literature
- Iconography of the Sistine Chapel
- Italian Politics
- Fathers and Godsons: The Mafia
- Corruption and Kickbacks in Italian Society
- Ethics and Batman
- Getting Around Florence
- Halloween Costume Party
- Florence Dance Theater: Lecture and Dance Demonstration
- Amnesty International: The Death Penalty
- Thanksgiving Dinner
- Presentation and Discussion of Franco Zeffirelli's ""Brother Sun, Sister Moon," the Life of St. Francis of Assisi
- Protestants in a Catholic Society
- Women in Italian Society
- Who's That in the Picture? Subject Matter in Italian Art
- So You're Thinking About Staying...
- Going Home Culture Shock
- End of the Semester Party

## Close-ups of A Few Students Gathered Around the Dining Table

**Karen Wardzala**, age 23, is working on an M.A. in Renaissance art history in the Syracuse University in Florence program. She has an undergraduate degree from Dickinson College.

*One of the attractions of Wednesday night suppers is that they are not school-related. This is a great place to meet people. The dinner is inexpensive and this is a nonthreatening atmosphere. Even if you speak Italian well, it's refreshing to step into a very American atmosphere.*

*Going abroad isn't for everybody. One thing almost everybody finds is that they learn as much about themselves as they learn about Italian culture. I've learned to put up with things I definitely wouldn't put up with in the States. It's expensive here and not having much money can really clarify your*

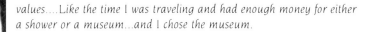

values....Like the time I was traveling and had enough money for either a shower or a museum...and I chose the museum.

**Cate Mellen**, age 24, is also a graduate of Dickinson College, studying art history.

*Living abroad gives you another outlook on American life and puts things in perspective. I've learned patience and I've become a more open, understanding person.*

*Everyone has their own personal perspective, but we encounter people every day whose national experiences are different than ours. I've learned that I can't say "Italians do this...Americans do that." The experience of living here helps you break down your stereotypes...all kinds of stereotypes everywhere.*

*We're challenged by the Italian language, but think of the Florentines, the people working at the train station, in the stores, in the market, in cafés, just walking down the street being asked directions by tourists. Florentines are constantly forced to respond to a dozen different languages every day of their lives.*

**Elizabeth Staley** is a 21-year-old senior from St. Olaf College.

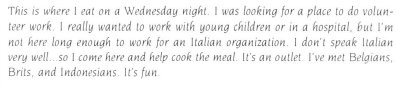

*This is where I eat on a Wednesday night. I was looking for a place to do volunteer work. I really wanted to work with young children or in a hospital, but I'm not here long enough to work for an Italian organization. I don't speak Italian very well...so I come here and help cook the meal. It's an outlet. I've met Belgians, Brits, and Indonesians. It's fun.*

**Joe Pettigrew** is an art history major at Carleton College. Joe does not attend services at his college chapel or in the Episcopal church in town, although he is an Episcopalian and attends his home church in San Diego (All Souls). In Florence he has joined the St. James choir and has brought six to seven others to sing with him. He has played the organ in a pinch. He feels more congregations ought to have similar college night programs.

*This is a great place to meet people from other colleges. It's good for people of the same age to come together, to find out about each other's country....The fellowship is good.*

*A program like this [St. James] is an excellent way to get young people excited about the church. Lots of people go to church as children. They rebel in their teens and may never go back. Programs like this could make them want to return.*

### The Value of International Youth from: A Leader's Perspective

Americans do not come to Florence to spend their time with other Americans. On the other hand, Florence is expensive; students don't have much money and so we try to give them a good, solid meal once a week. We don't say it in just so many words but we give these kids a shoulder to cry on.

Michelle [a New York attorney now living with her family in Florence] is an earth mother. She runs the kitchen and she finds that the students with the most yearning for Mom's kitchen, the ones that most need the extra support, will come early and help her cook the meal, and they'll talk while they peel the vegetables.

—Pamela Renai della Rena

## Serving Dinner, Feeding Souls

It's evangelistic. You can't hit kids on the head with the Bible. We give these kids a full meal, a place to talk to each other in a safe, happy community. Here students see little old ladies working for nothing. They see them doing something for others out of the goodness of their hearts. One action is worth more than a thousand words. Isn't that what the church should be? A place where people are fed and nurtured?

As Christians, we have a responsibility to our children. I'm not a counselor, but I hear all kinds of problems. I'm not asking them or telling them anything. I'm just providing them with a safe place where they feel secure.

To members of any church located in an area with a lot of students, I say DO IT! Start a program like this. This is the greatest age! These kids are smart and open. They are courageous. So many of them come from divorced parents. So many feel abandoned by their families. They are raising themselves. Yet, just the same, they are courageous enough to go abroad.

—Michele Spike, cook

Any time you stop being introspective or self-maintaining and start looking outward, then you start doing ministry. It becomes Christ's body reaching out to the stranger. This change from receiving to giving is a major transition in the spiritual life. Why do we celebrate tonight? Because we are all strangers in a strange land....

—the Rev. Peter Casparian, rector

## A Cook's Recipe for Success

1. Being substitute parents. The students like the camaraderie of the kitchen. It makes them feel as if they were at home.

2. We make everything from scratch, even grating the cheese. We have fresh vegetables that all have to be washed and sliced. In the USA, there is so much prepared and processed food, also parents are working without much time to prepare meals the old fashioned way. Lots of students come to learn how to cook.

3. The students feel at ease. They ask us lots of questions about Florence and share their impressions and insights.

4. I think we've found the right combination of program and dinner. The programs are varied and interesting and not related to their courses of study.

5. The meal is a real bargain at Lire 10,000 ($6.50).

6. The church atmosphere. The students may not say so, but I think they like it that the dinner is in a church, a church that is relaxed and welcoming to everybody.

—Sally Cook

## Job Descriptions

### Coordination

Responsibilities: call committee meetings, prepare meeting agendas, chair meetings, work up programs, make contacts with prospective speakers, evaluations, tabulate and distribute, meet with father, check to see how things are going in general, prepare the speaker, set up equipment for the speaker, order equipment, test equipment, see to special needs of the performers, call speaker to thank them, introduce speaker, organize students not working in the kitchen, make speaker comfortable, sell books, make rounds during evening to make sure all is running smoothly, make sure the staff is fed, replace staff when someone cannot make it, stand in place of other staff when they cannot make it, when changes are proposed, try to call around and get a sense of what the others think, get a general idea where the students are coming from, write minutes, have them xeroxed, distribute, oversee publicity: i.e. its design, addresses, mailing and distribution, prepare the budget, prepare requests for funding, get estimates for new equipment to be purchased. Number of staff needed: 3

### Dining Room

Responsibilities: set tables, newsletter, selling books, announcements, selling tickets, taking tickets, flyers distributed at dinners, announce menu, birthdays, keeping count of the students, give out name tags, greeting and farewell to students, Number of staff needed: 4

### Wine and Water

Responsibilities: order wine, bottle wine, order water , bottle water, rinse bottles, purchase corks, serve wine and water and clean up area. Number of staff needed: 3

### Kitchen

Responsibilities: order bread, order vegetables, grocery shop, purchase paper plates, spices, oil, vinegar, occasional equipment, oversee the crostone table, call tables up to be served, set up dishes and serving equipment, serve students, plan menu, coordinate serving of primo, secondo and desserts with the dining room, give tasks to student helpers, clean pots at the end of the meal, refill bread baskets. Number of staff needed: 7

### Clean-up

Responsibilities: clear tables, enlist student volunteers, supervise plate scraping, collect glasses, wine carafés, empty water bottles, dispose of food, collect and bundle garbage, wash table tops, put pots and flatware in soapy water. Number of staff needed: 3

### Vestry Representative

Responsibilities: represent the committee to the vestry, meet with other vestry committees on shared concerns, keep a general idea of how the ministry relates to other aspects of the church's activity and where possible, join these together.

## Background

St. James was left a small bequest specifically to help foster Italian/American student contacts in Florence. Over the years a number of ideas were tried, including the hiring of a part-time worker to make contact with students. Nothing really took off. Then in 1992, Christine Smith, then the director of Syracuse University's art history program in Florence, and Michele Spike, a transplanted New York lawyer, decided to try an evening dinner program. They assembled a small committee that included people in touch with the student community, not all of them members of St. James. Pamela Renai della Rena, for instance, had been assistant director of the University of Michigan's abroad program. She is an energetic woman used to working with students.

Christine served as chair, "the world's original organizer," according to Pamela. After a year, which some admit was sometimes a little chaotic, Christine suggested that each member of the committee take on a specific role and wrote job descriptions for: the coordinator, the head of the dining room, coordinators of wine and water, the kitchen, clean-up, and vestry representative.

Serving dinner to college students once a week was obviously a good idea. The first night, the committee thought maybe ten people would show up, but thirty came. The next week it was seventy. That number has been more or less constant ever since.

Committee members recruit students to assist them in their areas of responsibility, and they are very open to the students' suggestions, but students are not on the committee. This is because, unlike a college ministry program in the USA, where students are there for four years, these students are in Florence for only a semester or less. According to Michele Spike, "Every semester we create the core group."

Anyone who wants to help can find something to do, and International Youth has been blessed with some wonderful cooks, who have just appeared. Sally Cook recalls that one night Scott, a Lebanese-American showed up. He was a professional chef, who was working at a fish restaurant in

Venice three hours away. He heard about the program. Since his restaurant was closed Wednesdays, Scott came to Florence to cook at St. James.

The program began and continues as a lay initiative in the parish. It has been successful. It helps that the current rector of the parish, the Rev. Peter Casparian, had been a college chaplain at the University of Kansas (one of the chapters in this resource). Peter contributes his expertise in working with students. Through his helpful presence, he underscores the spirituality of the ministry, and gives words to its theological significance.

Students come the first time because they see the flier about the program included in each student's "Welcome to Florence Packet." It includes a small map showing St. James' location, a brief description of what International Youth is about, the day and time of the dinners, and the price and the title of each Wednesday night's program. Virtually every student coming to Florence receives such a packet. Students come back to International Youth and invite their friends because word travels quickly. Success breeds success.

## Things You Can't Leave Florence Without Having Seen...

The view from Fort Belvedere. San Miniato. Viveli's. Sunset in San Gimignano. The view from the tower of Palazzo Vecchio (the best place to say "good-bye" to Florence from, when that sad day arrives). The Boboli Gardens. The Bargello. The Central Market inside. The azaleas in bloom. The Medici Chapel. The restored Masaccios at the Church of the Carmine. The Campo in Siena. The Cinque Terre. At least one movie in Italian. The "Scoppio del Carro" on Easter Sunday. Fiesole—not just the town, but the hills around it. The traffic on the Viali. The Leaning Tower of Pisa (the only thing they will ask you about at home). The Mediterranean. Cypress trees. Piazza Santo Spirito. A Carabiniere in full-dress uniform. The Modern Art Gallery in Palazzo Pitti. A waiter peel and slice an orange in thirty seconds. The Science Museum in Palazzo dei Giudici. Donatello's David. The Laurentian Library. A bottle of great, extra-virgin olive oil. A soccer game. A first-class international train. The primroses and violets in bloom in the country. Water in the Arno. A "dry" wall. Piazza San Marco in Venice. Graffiti. Palazzo Vecchio illuminated on a holiday. The medieval streets around Santa Croce. Santa Croce. A rock concert. Carlie's Bakery. Mantova. Spaghetti alle vongole. The cats in Rome. Elizabeth and Robert Browning's house. The English cemetery. The Pergola Theater. The Tuesday morning "mercatino" at the Cascine. A full moon rising upstream over the river. The ugliest statue ever sculpted in Porta Romana. The lobby of the Excelsior. The "The Flood Reached Here" plaques. Bellosguardo. Gucci's price tags. Pigeons. Botticelli's Primavera. Primavera. Tourist buses. Pecorino cheese with bacilli. The Synagogue. Leather jackets. Silk underwear. The American flag at the Consulate. The pictures of nineteenth-century Florence at Alinari's. Wine flasks. Assisi. Rubbish. Gypsies. High Mass at the Duomo. Refugees. High school kids on "motorini." Red Ferraris. Bottled water. Geraniums on balconies. A crowded bus.

Add your own in the empty space. You will forget many of these things, and others of them you won't miss, but we hope you will never forget and always miss...Florence herself.

—Pamela Renai della Rena
*International Youth Bulletin*

# Last Words from the Guest Book

I'll miss you guys so much. Wednesday night was always "Church Supper Night." You took us in and were our friends, parents and meal ticket. You epitomize goodwill and friendship.

—*Nathan Becker, James Madison University*

I was really happy to have Passover at the church. It made it feel real and like I was at home.

—*Rob Newman, Richmond, VA*

You have been our family a million miles away!

—*Melanie Houst, Mechanicsville, VA*
—*Sybil Sheffield, Alexandria, VA*

I'll never forget those opera singers and ice cream sandwiches.

—*Ashley Poule, Raleigh, NC*

Food, love, caring...it brought back memories of home.

—*Emily King, Riverside, CT*

I'll give you credit for any future masterpieces I may create in the kitchen!

—*Andrea Casfugno*

The best welcome of all in Florence, which is saying something!

—*Ian Cockburn, Beckenham, Kent, England*

Your open and wholehearted hospitality—it is the true meaning of unconditional. When I came to Italy I was cold and hungry. When I came to "Church Dinners" on Wednesdays I was still cold but never hungry.

—*Michelle Jennings, James Madison University*

# Town, Gown, and Chapel

## A CAMPUS-BASED CONGREGATION

A pre-Revolutionary Anglican chapel on the hill gave Chapel Hill its name. So right from the start, the Episcopal Church has taken a formative role in this picturesque, university community of 44,000, nestled in North Carolina's rolling, wooded hills. Residents call it "The Southern Part of Heaven," a motto coined from the title of a book written by William Meade Prince who, as a young boy, played the organ at Chapel of the Cross.

The University of North Carolina opened its doors in 1795 as the first state university in the nation. University officials consider it one of the eight "Public Ivy" universities, offering an education comparable to that of Ivy League schools. In the early 1840s one of its professors, the Rev. William Mercer Green, decided that there ought to be an Episcopal church in the midst of the campus (the old Anglican chapel had long since disappeared) to serve the university's students, faculty, and staff. Thus, the Chapel of the Cross was built and Green became its first rector.

The Chapel of the Cross, which has 1,500 baptized members and four packed services every Sunday, is staffed by a rector and three full-time associates, plus several nonstipendiary clergy. Through its years of growth and change, it has never wavered from its primary focus as a campus-based congregation.

The Chapel of the Cross has sponsored probably the longest continuous ministry to students of any parish in the USA. So seriously has it taken its campus ministry that in 1919 the vestry forced the resignation of a rector because he was not visiting students enough. According to the Rev. Stephen Stanley, present associate for campus ministry and Episcopal chaplain at UNC, "Campus ministry is this parish's number one outreach. It's historically linked with the parish's identity."

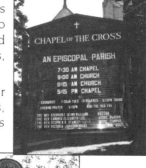

77

### Episcopal Campus Ministry

The Episcopal campus ministry is overseen by the parish's University Ministry Committee; the campus minister, the Rev. Stephen Stanley; and five chaplain's assistants. Young people meet in the Campus Center, an attractive large space with cozy alcoves and a kitchen, furnished with comfortable couches and over-sized armchairs. It is open every day until 10:00 in the evening, and students are always welcome to drop in, relax, study, or fix themselves a meal.

While the Anglican Student Fellowship (ASF), the student group for undergraduates, is the major focus of Chapel of the Cross's ministry to young adults, there is also another organization designed for young working adults and graduate students, the Graduate and Professional Fellowship (GPF).

In addition to participating in the programs and fellowship of these two groups, young people are welcome to take part in any of the parish's rich fare of courses, programs, projects, and ministries. Within these offerings there are several that appeal particularly to an intergenerational age range, mainly the parish Host Family Program and Habitat for Humanity.

For most of the young people, either ASF or GPF is the doorway to the church's other programs. However, others involve themselves directly in the parish through attending Sunday worship, teaching Sunday school, singing in the choir, or through study programs and parish projects. They may rarely or never go to ASF or GPF. Chapel of the Cross is large and varied enough to sustain all levels of need and interest. All that is missing is a racial/cultural mix. This writer questioned this and discovered that Chapel Hill is overwhelmingly white with European Americans making up 81 percent of the population, and African Americans, 12.6 percent. Nonetheless, leaders of the church are concerned about its lack of racial diversity, and have initiated a sister parish relationship with St. Paul AME Church, the oldest church attended by blacks in Chapel Hill. Also, the University of North Carolina takes seriously its role in helping African American students realize their potential. According to a *Journal of Blacks in Higher Education* survey, UNC has the third highest graduation rate for blacks of any state-supported university in the nation with 64 percent of its African American students graduating within six years (the average rate for black students graduating from college is less than 50 percent).

In describing UNC students, Bill Wells, Chapel of the Cross member and assistant director of the Office of Scholarships and Student Aid at the university, says,

> *Students are different now! They have a spiritual base. They are not shy about talking about their faith. Some of them don't believe but they don't mind being up front about it. They are overextended like their parents. They care about everything and they want to do everything. Their strength is that they care about something more substantial than houses, automobiles, and clubs.*

The Episcopal campus ministry is sponsored jointly by the Chapel of the Cross and the Diocese of North Carolina. Its annual budget in 1996 was $93,371, with the parish supplying about 60 percent of that, and the diocese 40 percent.

## Anglican Student Fellowship (ASF)

The ASF is the centerpiece of Chapel of the Cross's campus ministry. It is a university-recognized organization with faculty liaisons just like any other university association. Such recognition gives the Anglican Student Fellowship a standing not only in the church but in the university.

The chaplain oversees ASF in conjunction with five chaplain's assistants—called CAs—volunteer coordinators who are appointed every year. Each CA takes on one or more responsibilities for the overall organization of the Anglican Student Fellowship (ASF) such as food, finance, program, social events, outreach and mission, worship, and music.

Publicizing the Anglican Student Fellowship begins early. In the middle of the summer Stephen Stanley writes to all the Episcopal students telling them about ASF's activities. He introduces them to the up-coming year's CAs and invites them to "Welcome Week" at the beginning of the academic year. Welcome Week activities include a barbecue at the church for all the students, and a Labor Day weekend trip to the beach. Students also find out about ASF through freshmen orientation activities and through campus publications.

## Anglican Student Fellowship Programs and Activities

- **Beach Getaway**. A beginning of the school year, weekend beach trip to the North Carolina coast for students to get to know each other.

- **Weekly Tune-up.** Each Tuesday night the GSF sponsors informal worship at 5:30, with lots of music, and dinner at 6:30, cooked by members of the parish or the students.

- **Parish Host Family Program**. Parish members "adopt" a student for the year. The program is designed to help students become acquainted with parish individuals and families so they can experience a sense of the wider community while attending the university. The relationship may take any form that is mutually agreeable. It usually involve meals in parishioners' homes, attending social functions together, and providing a quiet place to study.

- **Alternate Spring Break**. Depending on the year, Alternate Spring Break may entail building houses for Habitat for Humanity or visiting the Diocese of North Carolina's Companion Diocese of Costa Rica.

- **Personal Counseling**. Counseling is available from the chaplain and Stephen Ministers, lay people in the congregation trained in counseling skills.

- **Vocational Mentoring**. Various parishioners who are also university faculty make themselves available to assist students in their areas of expertise.

- **A Chapel of the Cross University Student Guide**, available to each student, describes all parish programs, services, and activities. *The Anglo-File*, an ASF newsletter is produced every six weeks in the academic year by the chaplain's assistants. It contains details of timely events and news.

## Celebrations and Concerns

I think the best thing about ASF is "Celebrations and Concerns." As part of worship every week we go around the circle and everyone has the opportunity to say something they want to celebrate and something they are concerned about.

—Abbey Foster, chaplain's assistant

### Who's Who in the Campus Center...

**B. J. Owens**, age 21, is a senior majoring in history. He is the head chaplain's assistant.

*To me, this is one of the great lessons of college: challenge. Challenge what you know, try all kinds of new stuff, and above all, never stay in one place for too long.*

*Spiritually, I'm afraid I have no choice; what I experienced at school immediately shook the religious base I had thought would always support me. But I saw the world had changed; what I had previously believed did not make sense to me anymore. I would have liked to stay in one place on this one, but it was not meant to be. This has turned out to be a time to question, pray, and hopefully find a deeper spirituality that will carry me from this period of transition to the next.*

*ASF is an open community, which welcomes questions, challenges, and diversity. For some people, self-discovery occurs in the classroom, or perhaps even in a church. For others, it comes during late evenings with friends, or visits to the mountains. And for a few select idiots, it comes at 6:45 in the morning on the steps of the Lincoln Memorial, after an all-night drive from Chapel Hill to Washington, D.C. ASF strives to include all of these.*

**Julie Muñoz**, age 19, is a sophomore.

*It's hard to think about my faith and what I want to do with my life. Whenever there's a moment that's free (I am always busy!), my faith is the last thing that comes to my mind.*

*Now when I'm really stressed, when I'm really feeling pulled apart, it's a different story. Then I'm looking for something to steady me. That's when I start pulling my faith back from the corner of the closet where I keep it.*

**Rob Elliot**, age 19, is a sophomore majoring in environmental science. He is a chaplain's assistant.

*I didn't have a church attachment in high school, but my sister was at UNC and ASF was an important part of her life. I came my freshmen year, starting at the Beach Getaway, and I liked it. I've been here every Tuesday night ever since.*

*This is a safe place where the ideals of Jesus are put into practice. You feel comfortable here. No one's preaching at you.*

*I participate in the Host Family Program. Jean French is "Mom" to me and also to B.J. Last year I really wanted to go on the Goodwill Mission Trip to Costa Rica (Alternate Spring Break) and didn't have the money to go. I didn't say anything but Jean could tell I wanted to go, so she gave me the money. No one could ask for a better "Mom" than that!*

**Abbey Foster**, age 22, is a senior majoring in journalism. She is also a chaplain's assistant.

*I'm a cradle Episcopalian. Ever since junior high, I've been really involved in the Episcopal Church. It's important to me to keep up my faith. I'm always here on a Tuesday night. The Episcopal Campus Center is a place where people are really friendly. You can come here and worship and just be.*

**Matt Savage**, age 21, is a senior. He is a pre-dental and sociology major, and also a chaplain's assistant.

*ASF is something I can always count on to be there. It brings different kinds of people together to work and to become friends.*

## Essentials of Campus Ministry

1. Campus ministry has to be grounded theologically.

2. It has to be morally engaged in the issues of our time.

3. It has to be collegially led—clergy and laity, chaplains working along with the students.

4. Campus ministry needs broad structures of support so that its life is not dependent upon the person who happens to be the chaplain at the time.

5. It needs support from other denominational chaplains, the diocese, and other local parishes. Campus ministry needs many friends to succeed!

—the Rev. Stephen Stanley

## We Are Students!

We go to classes.
We read and absorb and are comprehensively tested on heavy amounts of various materials.
We sleep very little.
We drink ourselves into oblivion.
We kill ourselves with several types of smoke.
We cough and keep smoking. Someone is always sick. Someone is always complaining.
We become attached to close friends.
We smother each other.
We lean too much.
We think often of the past and want to go back. We know we cannot.
We all have separate lives, families, backgrounds, and pasts. We live totally different from how we used to live.
We are frustrated and sometimes want to give up, but we never stop trying.

We disregard health.
We eat awful foods.
We are forced to think about the future. We are scared and confused.

We reach out for things, yet we don't find them.
We try to sort out our minds, which are filled with studies, worries,
problems, memories, emotions—powerful feelings.
We wander the halls looking for happiness.

We hurt—a lot.

We keep going because, above all else, we never stop learning,
growing, changing, and most important, dreaming.
Dreams keep us going and they always will.
All we can do is be thankful that we have something to hold onto,
like dreams and each other.

—UNC student (anonymous)

## Graduate and Professional Fellowship (GPF)

The Graduate and Professional Fellowship consists of young
people from ages twenty to forty, single and married, graduate students,
nonstudents, working, looking for jobs. Most of them are in transition—
from undergraduate to graduate school, from university to first jobs,
from job to job, looking for jobs, looking for satisfying relationships. The
GPF exists to provide support and fellowship in a Christian setting for
young adults seeking to integrate their faith into their daily lives.

The mainstay of GPF is the monthly potluck dinner held in the Episcopal Campus Center the
first Friday of every month.

### Activities
• Spontaneous social activities
• Movies
• Baseball games
• Bowling
• Ice skating
• Weekend hikes
• A fall beach retreat
• Bible study
• Book study groups
• Wine tasting
• Dancing

### Service
• Food drives
• Sponsoring a foster child
• CROP Walk
• Volunteering in a center for adults
  with disabilities
• Cooking meals for AIDS patients
• Habitat for Humanity

## Why It Works

The education and service opportunities are what make
the GPF work because in them we have a place to begin. If this
were just a social group we would divide.

—Laura Rose, GPF coordinator

82

## Support—Within and Without

Campus ministry in Chapel Hill has many advocates. The Chapel of the Cross campus ministry is the most visible ministry of the parish and is structured to receive support from both within the parish and from the wider religious community of Chapel Hill.

### From Within...

The University Ministry Committee is composed of members of the parish and representatives of the young adult groups. Committee members serve as liaisons between the vestry and parish and the wider university community.

## What It Takes to Succeed in Campus Ministry:

1. An exciting core of dedicated and enthusiastic student leaders and, in the words of Jean DeSaix, a member of the University Ministry Committee, "one cheerleader, one student who can really motivate the others, at least once every three years."
2. Letting the students do it. Let them organize and manage the program.
3. A chaplain with lots of personal charisma.
4. Let everyone take charge of things at one time or another so that all participants take ownership of the group.
5. A comfortable, accessible place where young people can sit and "crash."
6. A strong communications network to keep everyone in touch.
7. Location. We're on the campus!
8. Strong diocesan and parish support. This is our parish's most visible outreach ministry.
9. Music—it's an integral part of ASF.

—Pooled from members of the University Ministry Committee

### An Episcopal Church Presence on the Campus is Critical

The Episcopal Church with its history of tradition having reason—with a capital R—has a call to be a presence on university campuses, especially where evangelical Protestants are clearly motivated to make themselves felt. To give up the campus to this branch of Christianity would be to give up a call to witness to another branch of the faith (i.e. Anglican tradition).

—the Rev. Lisa Fishbeck, chair,
Department of Campus Ministry, Diocese of North Carolina

### From Without...

Stephen Stanley, Episcopal chaplain, was a founding member and takes an active part in the Campus Ministers' Association (CMA). Composed of campus ministers from historic Jewish and Christian traditions, the CMA is committed to ministry to and with the university community. It encourages interfaith action in addressing pertinent issues of campus and community life.

Acting together, the various denominational campus ministers are seen as advocates for a healthy campus environment that respects and values the legacies of diverse religious traditions.

The day before the visit of this writer, CMA campus ministers were planning to give a presentation, entitled "Faith Development on the Campus," to members of the university's Student Support Services (representatives from Housing, Orientation, Crisis Services, Counseling, Student Health, the Dean of Students, etc.). The questions for small group discussion listed below, were devised by Sister Margaret Harig of the Newman Catholic Student Center. They would be helpful in initiating a dialogue on religion at any campus.

### Faith Development on the Campus

—Could you share any knowledge you have of departments, courses, programs, or support services at the university that have as their mission the faith development of students?

—Do you believe that the university has any responsibility to foster the faith development of students? If "ethical/moral learning" were substituted for "faith development," would you respond differently?

—Do you have any knowledge of the resources that students most frequently rely on in times of personal crisis, loss, celebration, depression, or when making life choices?

—What is your impression of the role played by religious/faith traditions in influencing students' lives during their years at the university?

—Do you see any trends in the growing or diminishing role of faith traditions as part of the holistic or liberal arts education of students?

## Out into Regions Beyond—Putting Faith into Action

Town, gown, and chapel—this is the three-legged stool that defines Chapel Hill. The Chapel of the Cross has been a part of it all from the beginning. Its Episcopal campus ministry, long established and well-known, does not rest on its laurels. Many lives of faith in action have been, and continue to be, nurtured in this parish's historic outreach to the university community. But the acid test of any ministry is how much of it shows outside its hallowed walls; how much it has been the building blocks constructing strong, deep, sturdy, and responsible Christian lives; how much is taken out into the regions beyond—in the lives and actions of its participants—into the community, the nation and the world. Episcopal campus ministry does well in the test, as the following two profiles illustrate.

**Joanne Werdel**, age 21, is an English major. She agrees to an interview, but she's in a hurry. She is rushing off to Carrboro to teach a class in English as a second language. Most of her students are Hispanic. For next year she's thinking about applying to the Peace Corps, or Teach for America, a federal program to place recent college graduates in urban settings that have a tough time attracting teachers.

> *Right now I'm trying to help the housekeepers, who are fighting the university's efforts to privatize housekeeping. I'm helping them work for better working conditions. Also at stake is the issue of racism and sexism—90 percent of the housekeepers are black, 76 percent of them women. They're asking for the same basic rights everyone else wants. Why am I doing it? It's the right thing to do.*

**Ramsay Hoke**, age 24, is a 1995 UNC graduate who served as a chaplain's assistant, and also head CA. Ramsay works as an interpreter and teacher of English as a second language under the auspices of AmeriCorps (see sidebar in The Episcopal Church Welcomes You chapter). He spent last year in Costa Rica as a Volunteer for Mission.

I wanted to leave America for an extended period to see how other people live. I wanted to learn for myself how they live in Latin America. I worked in Costa Rica with youth from September 1995 to August 1996.

I learned the language in the street from the kids. I worked at a day care center (community center) as a tutor in geography, history, and math. I played basketball with the kids.

Believe me, I learned a lot. There's not a lot of money in Costa Rica. The people don't have much materially—no cars, no luxuries—but they dress nicely. My friends were making $350 a month and they felt lucky to have jobs. Women are working in the factory for that and supporting four to five children at home.

Family is much stronger with them than I had experienced here. And they also have a sense of place—my town, my relatives—these are important to them.

The experience has affected me. I see Americans alienated from everything—alienated from family, alienated from friends, alienated from themselves. Also they're into doing, whereas in Costa Rica they're into being. They are more content to relax, to take their time to solve their problems. They tolerate more and seem to have more fun. They love dancing. The party starts when it starts and it never ends. Here everyone's just too busy to take the time.

An experience like this can be hard and lonely, but I'd recommend it. For the first three months I felt like I had no place. I felt maybe I should go back to the States. I got robbed at gun point. It was tough, but I had two friends who were godsends.

Every American needs to know what is going on in the rest of the world. I can't say enough about the experience, just the way it makes you think and feel differently. You can't gauge what's going on until you see the world in another context, from another perspective. It wakes you up to realize the effect the US has on other countries—politically, economically, socially....

Ramsay is walking in the shoes of others before him who have been a part of Episcopal campus ministry at the University of North Carolina. There is a saying in the Tao Teh Ching that "A journey of a thousand miles starts where your feet are." The feet of many who once walked into the Campus Center have continued walking on. And so they continue the journey they started at the chapel on the hill.

# Let
# The Son Shine

## DIOCESAN COMMUTER CAMPUS MINISTRIES

Everything went up in flames. It was on the eve of Thanksgiving that a fire swept through the downstairs of St. Mark's Church and consumed all the parish meeting rooms. When it had run its course only the walls were left standing. Included in the loss was the Canterbury Room, which only three weeks before had been painted and redecorated by the Southwest Texas State University (SWT) students who make up the San Marcos Canterbury. Resting in the ash were just a few remains—the shell of a refrigerator, the springs of a couch, a pair of twisted metal shelves, part of the television. What else lay hidden there? What voices spoke from the silence of the hollow? What parts of themselves lay buried in the veil of soot? What dreams, what hopes?

As the students gazed into the dark cavern of what had been their drop-in and meeting center, they expressed a mixture of shock, bewilderment, anger, grief, and determination to rebuild. To student peer minister, James Derkits, a 19 year-old sophomore, this was the first real loss he had sustained in his life, and it hurt.

So one week later when this writer visited, sharing reactions to the fire was the program for the evening. Meeting in a student center close to the church, the Rev. Bruce Wilson, rector of St. Mark's, and Susan Hanson, director of the Canterbury Program, tried to help the students deal with the loss through reflection, the evening's liturgy, and by listening to each other. Susan introduced the process:

*Every loss like this reminds us of every other loss we've sustained in our lives. We have to find the Cross again in the middle. What we learn is that we can lose things that we love, which are very important to us, and that the loss won't kill us. We're still here.*

Bruce passed around slips of paper in various colors and asked the students, either alone or with a neighbor, to think about the meaning of the fire and to "Write down anything you wish—your hopes, your anger, your sorrow. Or, just leave it a blank page." Silence fell upon the room. After fifteen to twenty minutes the slips were gathered and they became the offering of the Eucharist. Bruce raised the bowl with the words, "We don't know what the future holds but we know who holds the future."

## Campus Ministry in the Diocese of West Texas

St. Mark's, San Marcos, is one of the four campus ministry centers of the Diocese of West Texas. It is located in the center of the Southwest Texas State University campus. Its location is cited as one factor contributing to the strong Canterbury program. Another is that almost all the members are students at Southwest Texas State University (SWT). The other well-established Canterbury is in San Antonio, where it draws students from seven campuses with most of them coming from the University of Texas at San Antonio (UTSA), Trinity University, San Antonio College, Palo Alto College, and St. Mary's University. This group meets in the Chapel House located on the grounds of the Diocesan Center in central San Antonio. Both programs were visited in connection with this project. Two other Canterbury programs are located in parishes close to campuses in Edinburg and in Corpus Christi. A few of the students who attend Canterbury live in dormitories, but most of them live at home with parents, or rent apartments with friends, and commute to school.

Each of the four centers is served by a part-time chaplain, who is rector of the church where Canterbury meets, or by a director of Canterbury, as well as from one to three student peer ministers. Student peer ministers work ten hours a week. They publicize Canterbury programs on their respective campuses, arrange transportation to meetings where necessary, and visit and follow-up students who come. Student peer ministers are trained locally by either the chaplain or director of Canterbury,

and also at a diocesan retreat for peer ministers on a weekend at the beginning of the academic year. They are paid $250 a month for their work.

Campus ministry in the Diocese of West Texas is supervised by Mr. Ripp Hardaway, the diocesan Director of Youth Ministries. It is a newly defined job and he is new in it. Hardaway's responsibilities also include supervising camping and conferences. From 1990-95, the Rev. Doug Earle was full-time diocesan Coordinator for College Ministry.

By age, philosophy and theology, Earle and Hardaway are quite different. Earle could be considered a classic Episcopal college chaplain—broad theologically, eager to encourage deep questioning of the faith, challenging and intellectually rigorous. Hardaway is a 26 year-old layman who gained his experience coming up through parish and diocesan youth ministry and camping programs. The gospel came alive to him through his participation in Happening, a renewal weekend for high school students. He also wants to challenge students and make them think, but in different ways.

We visited at a time of changing leadership, thus the shape of the diocese's campus ministries is still in flux, but whatever personality or style it takes on, one thing is guaranteed: it will have the full support of the bishop, the Rt. Rev. James Folts. Bishop Folts was rector of St. Mark's, San Marcos from 1968-79, when the plan of using students as peer ministers was initiated at Southwest Texas State University. He credits the Rev. Canon David Veal, then diocesan Coordinator of Campus Ministries, with the idea.

Bishop Folts acknowledges many ups and downs in the area of campus ministry over the years. "It suffers today as a result of a steady neglect over the past fifteen to twenty years." But he's optimistic about the future:

*This is an area of ministry that is of vital importance. We must reclaim our ministry on college and university campuses. We're intent on doing that in the Diocese of West Texas.*

Although the Diocesan Center is currently the meeting place for the San Antonio Canterbury, Bishop Folts would like to see all the campus ministries located in the parochial context; that is, using nearby parishes as gathering places for students, as is the case in San Marcos. It is his opinion that, "The parish, rather than a free-standing campus ministry center, gives student ministry stability and continuity."

Campus ministry in the Diocese of West Texas is unique in several ways. As already cited, most of the students are commuters. In addition, the majority of them have been Episcopalians all their lives. They have come to college Canterbury associations after having participated in strong parish and diocesan youth ministry programs as children and youth. The progression of Chris Little, a 19 year-old freshman at UTSA and a member of the San Antonio Canterbury, is typical: "I've done youth groups in my parish and when I went to college I couldn't see stopping it. So I came to Canterbury."

The further south one goes in Texas, the more Hispanic the population becomes. In the communities we visited, about half the 30,000 people in San Marcos are Hispanic; 56 percent of San Antonio's population of 1.9 million is Hispanic. The public universities and colleges in both cities mirror the cultural mix. The Canterburys do not. We were told that this is a matter of concern among diocesan leaders.

All four campus ministry centers have programs shaped by their respective customs, traditions, and interests. In each case the chaplain (local rector), or Canterbury director plans the program in conjunction with the student peer ministers. The usual weekly program will consist of worship, a meal prepared by parishioners, and a meeting with program. Weekend activities are also scheduled according to the interests of members.

### Local Canterbury Activities
• Camping
• Hiking
• Tubing on the Guadeloupe River
• Parties
• Going out to dinner at local restaurants
• Attending sports events
• Beach parties
• A "Random Act of Kindness Night"
• Movie night
• Country and Western dancing
• Cookouts
• Message therapist: tips on how to relax
• Time management
• Questions and answers with the bishop
• Labyrinth

On occasion one or more local Canterburys will cooperate on a project or activity. For example, the San Antonio Canterbury has planned a beach party and asked the Corpus Christi group to arrange accommodations close to the beach.

Community
Activities
New friendships
Teaching of the Word
Enrichment in Christ
Retreats
Belonging
Understanding
Real World
Years of memories

### Diocesan College Programs

Each local Canterbury is enhanced by diocesan programs for college and university students. The main ones are:

- Fall and Spring college conferences with speakers and activities.
- Vocaré, renewal weekends for college students.
- Weekends away.
- The Province VII event.

## Focus on the San Antonio Canterbury

(The Episcopal Students Association of San Antonio)

Ripp Hardaway coordinates the San Antonio Canterbury with the help of three student peer ministers: Elizabeth Bush, Charles Youngson, and Amanda Odeh. Charles goes to Trinity University, and Elizabeth and Amanda, the University of Texas at San Antonio (UTSA).

The T-shirt designed by Elizabeth Bush describes the San Antonio Canterbury in just a few words: community, activities, new friendships, teaching of the Word, enrichment in Christ, retreats, belonging, understanding the real world, and years of memories. Many of the students have been friends for years through parish and diocesan youth programs.

## Random Acts of Kindness Night—San Antonio's Best Program of the Year

We spread out over town. Some of us went to the supermarket and helped people carry their groceries. Some went to the laundromat and helped fold clothes. Someone went to the bus stop and talked to people as they waited for the bus to take them home from work. Someone else went to the library to help an old lady check out her books. Afterwards we came back and shared our experiences with each other.

—Amanda Odeh, student peer minister

## Who Makes It Happen?

**Charles Youngson**, age 21, is a student at Trinity University and a student peer minister.

*I believe that the Canterbury program is really becoming a place where college students can unite and worship God together in a relaxing atmosphere away from the rigors of university life.*

*I feel that I have been able to establish a fairly close relationship with each person who comes to Canterbury from Trinity. I frequently stop to chat with them on campus, inquire about their concerns with college life, tell them what went on at Canterbury if they had to miss, and in general treat them as friends in Christ, which they are. They have, in turn, been bringing friends with them, which I think is the best way to make the program grow.*

**Julie Cannaday**, age 24, is just about to graduate from SWT with a degree in early childhood education. Julie has been a student peer minister in San Marcos, but now she usually attends the San Antonio group, since she's doing her student teaching in San Antonio.

*I didn't pledge to a sorority, but I was looking for a community of people who had the same beliefs and were interested in the same things I am.*

*The home-cooked meal is a big attraction. All you can eat for $1! You can't beat it. I met one of my best friends through Canterbury. Canterbury brought* us together. At Canterbury we can "let down our guard." Here I can be free to let people know who I really am.

College is especially difficult the first year and people are looking for a place where they can fit in. Canterbury is so open and friendly, they can fit in here.

It's nice to be with a group of people struggling with what I am—in school, in relationships, with God, with career choices.

Hopes and dreams? I'd like to be a good teacher. I'd like to be able to change someone's life and maybe prevent them from going down the wrong track. Maybe in twenty years one of my students will remember that Miss Cannaday will have been that important teacher in the life of at least one child. I'd also like to get married and have a family of my own. I hope this is something God has in store for me.

## Faces in the San Antonio Crowd

—Chris Little

—Ben Houck and Stew Facile

## Quotable Quotes

"The most important thing is to keep an open mind, open heart, open door. College students need that and also knowing that someone really cares."
—Julie Cannaday, SWT senior

"You take someone who arrives at a university with a juvenile faith....The chaplain's task is to challenge it, to stretch it and make it grow so it will be strong enough to sustain them for the tough times in life ahead."
—the Rev. Doug Earle, member of the Commission on Ministry in Higher Education, and formerly diocesan Coordinator for College Ministry

"This generation of young people is looking for a place to belong—not a philosophy."
—Ripp Hardaway, Director of Youth Ministries

## Focus on the St. Mark's, San Marcos Canterbury

Let the Son Shine—"This is what the church is to me," according to Laura Keelan, the 21-year-old Southwest Texas State University (SWT) student who designed the San Marcos Canterbury T-shirt.

Laura explains that James Derkits, one of the student peer ministers, was looking through the prayer notebook in the Canterbury Room one day and saw in it the simple prayer—"Let the Son shine." It really spoke to them. They cut out a yellow spiral sun and the letters and made a mobile. Laura drew what she saw for a T-shirt design. The words have now become the motto of the San Marcos Canterbury. In Laura's words,

*When I think of Canterbury I think of the people and they reflect what Canterbury is about. It is being together and sharing our experiences, sharing our good times, sharing our walk with Christ.*

Virtually all of the San Marcos members are students at SWT. This provides a common shared experience. The Canterbury Room at St. Mark's Church was a drop-in center where students could freely come and go anytime; a comfortable place where they could relax and hang around. This is why the fire, mentioned at the start of this chapter, was so significant. It destroyed their home away from home. Susan Hanson, an instructor at SWT and a columnist for a local newspaper, *the San Marcos Record*, serves as the director of St. Mark's Canterbury. St. Mark's rector, the Rev. Bruce Williams, is chaplain. Peer ministers are James Derkits, a 19-year-old sophomore, and Lisa Charette, a 21-year-old graduating senior.

## The Labyrinth—San Marcos Canterbury's Best Program of the Year

We made a labyrinth with tape on the floor. It was dark and we lit candles and incense sticks. Chant music played in the background. This created a dim and mellow atmosphere. People prayed and prepared themselves for the walk. I told them to go when they felt ready. We waited until everyone had reached the middle and then we had a Eucharist in the middle of the labyrinth.

—James Derkits, student peer minister

## Who Makes It Happen?

**Lisa Charette,** age 23, a senior, is a student peer minister.

*This is a community that's open to people. They are a great joy to be with. The commitment of the members makes anything we do a great program.*

*I'm leaving but I hope everyone here will remember their faith in God and each other. It is faith that gets us through and helps each one of us find the path God has set out for us.*

**Isaiah Lewallan,** age 18, is a freshman majoring in geography.

*Canterbury is a new thing for me. I grew up a Baptist and I just stumbled in one day. I was impressed with the incredible love and warmth everyone here has for each other.*

**James Derkits,** age 19, is a sophomore from Silsbee, Texas. He is a student peer minister.

*This Canterbury has a small church family feeling, just like Silsbee. I got so much out of it last year, I felt so welcomed. I wanted to become a peer minister so I could give that same feeling to other people.*

*Our programs are planned by everyone—not just the peer ministers—so we have broad participation. Everyone feels involved and included.*

*I'd like to go to seminary. I feel I've been called; it's a calling I've felt all my life. I really started thinking about this when I was in high school. I think I have the gifts.*

**Susan Hanson,** director of St. Mark's Canterbury.

*I came to St. Mark's as a student twenty-five years ago. St. Mark's was important to me during those college years and I want the current students to have the same positive feelings.*

*Most of our students are Episcopalians. They come from all over Texas. Some have been involved in church camps. At Canterbury they're looking for community, for friendship. New freshmen want something to connect with.*

*We get between twenty and thirty at meetings. The group has to be a certain size to generate its own momentum and energy. Students are busy people. They're going to school; many are working. I'm concerned that we make the most of the time we have together.*

*We have a new rector and the students really like his interactive sermons. It gives them a chance to get connected.*

## Faces in the San Marcos Crowd

—Jerry Borchard, age 21, junior

—Mike Whitten, age 30, a part-time SWT student, full-time worker at Taco Bell

—Peer ministers: Lisa Charette, age 23; James Derkits, age 19; with Susan Hanson, Canterbury director

—The community sending off graduating senior, Lisa Charette

## Letting the Son Shine

Looking ahead, the students are expectant. Peer minister James Derkits said, "We now have a new project to rebuild our home. We'd just finished repainting and redecorating the Canterbury Room, so we know what we're doing." Everyone seems determined to continue to "Let the Son shine."

## The Making of a Youth/Young Adult Ministry Director

Just as many of the college and university students who participate in the college programs of the Diocese of West Texas have come up the route of parish and diocesan youth ministries, so it is with the new diocesan director of youth ministries. Ripp Hardaway was, in his own words, "Born and raised in church and it's just something I did on Sunday morning." But faith only really became alive to him in a personal way when he participated in Happening (high school Cursillo) in March, 1987.

*Through the course of the weekend I realized that Jesus Christ came for me personally. It was a combination of the talks and the community. The community was one of such love and acceptance...it was what Christ would want us to be. Every Sunday since then has become a celebration of that.*

*I was then asked to staff the next Happening and that really got me going. It gave me the opportunity to serve and through it I found that Christ's love is even more awesome when you're able to give it to others.*

Hardaway has a B.A. in psychology from Texas A. and M. University and is currently working on an M.A. in marriage and family therapy. He feels that being close in age to the students is an advantage in that he has grown up under some of the same influences. He says,

*This generation is hungry for relationships. So many of our peers come from single parent homes and, even if both parents are home, they're both working. They're too busy for their kids. Parents aren't home the way they used to be and students really feel it.*

*In the college years most students make a new set of friends. They get into new activities and establish new identities. We help the students when we invite them into welcoming, open, comfortable environments.*

*I'd like to see Canterbury students work to establish relationships with people outside of Canterbury—to spend time together, support one another and show they really care. Supporting one another and sharing life's experience—this would make a world of difference in people's lives.*

*This is what young people need to develop an active relationship with Christ: 1) an atmosphere of hospitality, 2) unconditional love, and 3) an environment where they can share their opinions without being condemned.*

## And Finally....Why do we do it?

### Why do we do it?

It's late afternoon when I bring my coffee and notepad out to the back porch of the retreat house where I've come for a short reprieve, and later still when I begin wrestling with the question that was put to me weeks before.

### Why do I work with the young people?

As a woman who teaches English half-time at the local university and writes for a third of my time for a small daily newspaper, I obviously had no need for a third part-time job. And yet, twelve months ago, when I was invited to step in as director of the Episcopal Campus Ministry at Southwest Texas State University, I didn't hesitate to accept. Why?

The simplest answer, I suspect, lies somewhere in my own history. As a transfer student entering this same university twenty-five years before, I had found my way to Canterbury very much in need of what it had to offer—a place where I could ask my questions, think seriously about my faith, and begin to live into a mystery much larger than I had ever imagined. Canterbury quickly became my home as a student, and in the spring of my junior year, I was confirmed in the Episcopal Church.

Yet another easy answer appeals to my utilitarian and practical side. As humdrum as it may sound, to work with college students is to invest in the future of our church. Looking back at the records of our programs, I find that seven of the student peer ministers who served between 1973 and the present have gone on to seminary. Far more are lay leaders in their own parishes, and some are now themselves the parents of active Canterburians. Put another way, to shortchange our ministry on the college campus is not only to opt out of one of our greatest opportunities as a church; it is, in effect, to invite our own demise.

Answers? Yes, but only of a sort. My real motive, I am beginning to believe, has more to do with this back porch view and far less with any reasons I've explored thus far.

Two days after Christmas, the air of the diocesan camp in the Texas Hill County is crisp and quiet, save for the twitter of the titmice and the raucous calls of flickers crisscrossing the field to my north. Already, white-tailed deer are gathering just beyond the fence, grazing in groups of two or three. Soon, as the light begins to fade, they will be moving out of their protective cover into the open to feed.

What I am witnessing, quite simply, is life on the margin, life in that in-between place where wood and field come together. My years of watching the creatures of the natural world have taught me that by waiting here, I'm likely to encounter far more life, far more comings and goings, than I'm apt to see either deep in the woods or walking through the open field. The marginal world is a world rich in texture and sound, a world filled with surprise.

**Why do I do it?**

For me, college ministry is just such a marginal world. It is a place where doubt and certainty collide, where what has "always been" is tested against multiple visions of what might be. In this marginal world where church and university are sometimes allies, sometimes foes, nothing, it seems, is set. Just as the students feel their own identities shifting beneath them, they sense that their concepts of God are changing as well. In this marginal world where all is flux, honesty and humor become virtues; faith becomes essential; life becomes very, very interesting.

Writing of her experiences working in the place where land and sea connect, biologist Rachel Carson once noted that this is a world that "keeps alive the sense of continuing creation and of the relentless drive of life." Working and worshiping in that marginal world known as campus ministry, I have felt the same. Amid the flux, amid the joy and confusion, amid the candor and the laughter, the Spirit is very much alive.

—Susan Hanson

About the authors......


Thomas K. Chu is the coordinator for young adult and higher education ministries at the Episcopal Church Center.

Sheryl A. Kujawa is the youth ministries coordinator, and the program director for ministries with young people at the Episcopal Church Center.

Anne Rowthorn is a writer, lecturer, and professional interviewer. Two of her most recent books are *The Liberation of the Laity* and *Caring for Creation*.

# SELECTED READING LIST

*This listed is not intended to be exhaustive, but to give the reader a sense of some of the works available pertaining to the evangelization of youth and young adults.*

Atkinson, Harley. *Handbook of Young Adult Religious Education*. Birmingham: Religious Education Press, 1995.

Brennan, Patrick. *Full Cycle Youth Evangelization: A Resource for Youth Ministries*. Allen, Texas: Tabor, 1993.

*Called to Teach and Learn: A Catechetical Guide for the Episcopal Church*. New York: The Episcopal Church Center, 1994.

Carey, George. *Spiritual Journey: 1,000 Young Adults Share the Reconciling Experience of Taize with the Archbishop of Canterbury*. Harrisburg: Morehouse Publishing, 1994.

Carmody, Denise Lardner Carmody. *Organizing a Christian Mind: A Theology of Higher Education*. Valley Forge: Trinity Press International, 1996.

Clement, Shirley F. and Thomas L. Salsgiver. *Youth Ministry and Evangelism: New Wine for a New Day*. Nashville: Discipleship Resources, 1991.

Daloz, Laurent A., et al. *Common Fire: Lives of Commitment in a Complex World*. Boston: Beacon Press, 1996.

Garber, Julie, ed. *Ministry with Young Adults: The Search for Intimacy*. Elgin: Faith Quest, Brethren Press, 1992.

Gribbon, Robert. *Developing Faith in Young Adults*. Washington: Alban Institute, 1992.

Gura, Carol and Carol Koch. *Ministering to Young Adults: A Resource Manual*. Winona: St. Mary's Press, 1987.

Harris, Maria. *Proclaim Jubilee: A Spirituality for the Twenty-First Century*. Louisville:Westminster John Knox Press, 1996.

Howe, Neil and Bill Strauss. *13th Generation: Abort, Retry, Ignore, Fail?* New York: Vintage, 1993.

Hughes, Amanda Millay and David E. Crean. *The Journey to Adulthood: A Parish Program of Spiritual Formation for Young People*. LeaderResources, 149 Dewberry Drive, Suite 101, Hockessin, DE 19701-2121.

Jones, Reginald L, ed. *Black Adolescents*. Berkeley: Cobb and Henry Publishers, 1989.

Kujawa, Sheryl A. and Lois Sibley, eds. *Resource Book for Ministries with Youth and Young Adults in the Episcopal Church*. New York: The Episcopal Church Center, 1995.

Loeb, Paul Rogat. *Generation at the Crossroads: Apathy and Action on the American Campus*. New Brunswick: Rutgers University Press, 1994.

Mahedy, William and Janet Bernardi. *A Generation Alone*. Downer's Grove: Intervarsity Press, 1994.

Males, Mike A. *The Scapegoat Generation: America's War on Adolescents*. Monroe: Common Courage Press, 1996.

Mitchell, Susan. *The Official Guide to the Generations*. Ithaca: New Strategist Publications, 1995.

Office of Evangelism Ministries. *The Catechumenal Process: Adult Initiation and Formation for Christian Life and Ministry*. New York: The Church Hymnal Corporation, 1990.

Parks, Sharon. *The Critical Years: Young Adults and the Search for Meaning, Faith and Commitment*. New York: HarperCollins, 1986.

Peters-Pries, Pam. *Living Unplugged: Young Adults, Faith and the Uncommon Life*. Newton: Faith and Life Pres, 1996.

*Plumbline: A Journal of Ministry in Higher Education*. The Episcopal Church at Northwestern University, 2010 Orrignton Avenue, Evanston, IL 60201-2912.

Portaro, Sam. *Conflict and a Christian Life*. Harrisburg: Morehouse Publishing, 1996.

Portaro, Sam and Gary Peluso. *Inquiring and Discerning Hearts: Vocation and Ministry with Young Adults on Campus*. Alpharetta: Scholars Press, 1993.

Prophets of Hope Editoral Team. *Evangelization of Hispanic Young People*. Winona: St. Mary's Press, 1995. (Available in Spanish and English)

Prophets of Hope Editorial Team. *Hispanic Young People and the Church's Pastoral Response*. Winona: St. Mary's Press, 1994. (Available in Spanish and English)

Shelton, Charles. *Adolescent Spirituality: Pastoral Ministry for High School and College Youth*. New York: Crossroad, 1989.

Ward, Pete. *Worship and Youth Culture: A Guide to Alternative Worship*. London: Marshall Pickering/HarperCollins, 1993.

Ward, Pete. *Youth Culture and the Gospel*. London: Marshall Pickering/HarperCollins, 1992.

Warren, Michael, ed. *Readings and Resources in Youth Ministry*. Winona: St. Mary's Press, 1987.

Winter, Gibson. *America in Search of Its Soul*. Harrisburg: Morehouse Publishing, 1996.

*Youth A Part: Young People and The Church*. London: National Society/Church House Publishing, 1996.